This book belongs to:

....

And if found, please contact

E-mail address:

....

Telephone No.

....

Fax No.

....

Postal Address:

....
....
....
....

ABOUT THE AUTHOR

Craig Hill has been involved with the travel industry for fifteen years. He first headed overseas in 1989 via the USA and eventually into Europe where he began working as a European coach driver with one of the major holiday companies specializing in eighteen to thirty five year old group travel. Between seasons he spent much of his time travelling through the USA, Canada, Egypt, Israel, Africa, New Zealand and Australia.

In 1996 he began conducting open age group tours through the main body of Central and Eastern Europe where he still mainly works today.

He has conducted tours ranging anywhere from two to seventeen countries per tour.

Areas visited on these tours have ranged from Great Britain to Turkey, Spain to the Czech Republic, and Israel, Egypt and Greece.

He is still very much involved with the travel industry and is now offering free lance tour directing services within the main areas of the European Union.

If you would like to comment on the contents of this book or have any suggestions for improving it, contact the author at craighill65@hotmail.com

EUROPE -

COACH TOURING AND TRAVEL JOURNAL

A Complete Guide

Craig Hill

KANUKA
PRESS

First published in New Zealand in 2004 by
KANUKA PRESS
18 Folkestone Drive, Hastings
NEW ZEALAND.

Copyright © 2004 Craig Hill

ISBN 0-9582519-0-8

Cover design by Mark Harvey.
Book design and production by Natalie Mitchell.
Printed and bound by Rush Printing Limited, Hastings.

ACKNOWLEDGEMENTS

To my mum and dad who possibly created in me the desire to travel with all the caravanning and camping holidays when I was young. I still remember crossing the dirt roads of the Nullabor Plain where the temperature sometimes reached 42 degrees centigrade, or in Fahrenheit, very, very, hot. The 3000km journey from Adelaide to Perth was usually undertaken in an un-airconditioned 1967 HR Holden with all the windows painted with tennis shoe white in order to stop the sun cooking my sister Lorraine, my brother Chris and myself to a crisp.

You would think that somehow this would have put me off travelling for life. But it didn't. Because looking back at the photos I realized that it is the adventure of the journey that really matters, and not so much the arriving.

I would also like to thank my friend Andrea very much. She encouraged me to stop talking about this book, and to actually get on and write it. Thanks also to her two girls Natasa and Vanda Lucuska who have made me laugh to the point of pain with some of their antics over the last few years.

To my surrogate parents Peter and Nannette, I am also grateful for welcoming me into their home in New Zealand and for treating me like one of their family. I am thankful to them also for introducing me to John the editor, without whom this book may not yet have been printed, and would still be inside me creating havoc trying to get out. My dream has become a reality. Thank you John.

Thanks to all the people I've worked with too. These include tour directors, drivers, suppliers, stopover staff, management and office support staff, and all the peripheral staff, most of whom would agree with me that anyone working in the hospitality or European coach travel industry sees life on the road as providing some of the greatest times of their life. Some of the memories gained along they can even share with their family and friends without being locked up, or frowned upon by society, or divorced by their partners.

Special thanks to Peter B. and Peter R. who gave me great encouragement and inspiration to become a tour director. Something to do with broccoli for brains, I think was the comment.

And to the clients I have shown through Europe over the years, and for the feedback they have given me, which has been the inspiration for the writing of this book. I hope you find that the information in these pages, and the personal journal section, fulfills the needs of both yourselves and your friends on your future travel journeys, sharing your experiences with others later will add a new dimension to your life, and give you more to offer people you meet in years to come. Thank you for travelling in the past, and it would be great to see you again in the future. Please encourage as many people as possible to get out and do the same. Leave the safety of the harbour.

Thank you all,
Craig

Further copies of this book can be obtained from the author at <u>craighill65@hotmail.com</u> *or from the publisher at* <u>natmitchell@xtra.co.nz</u>

TABLE OF CONTENTS

ACKNOWLEDGEMENTS _____5

PREFACE _____11

INTRODUCTION _____13

HOW TO WRITE YOUR OWN TRAVEL JOURNAL ___15

1 TRAVEL IN GENERAL _____17

What is travel? _____17

Why do we travel? _____18

The types of people who generally travel.. _____24

The different ways to travel. _____34

Different times to travel. _____50

Homesickness; how to minimize and prevent it. _____57

2 PICKING A PRODUCT _____59

The cost of a tour and where does the money go. _____59

Coach touring and what are the differences. _____62

Choosing the right tour. _____67

Things to trip you up. _____72

Incidental tour expenses. _____73

Budgeting on holiday. _____87

Choosing a travel agent. _____90

3 PREPARING TO GO AWAY _____92

Before you leave home. _____94

The countdown. _____ 97

Packing Tips. _____ 111

Getting to the airport. _____ 112

4 YOU'RE ON YOUR WAY _____ 114

Arrival at the first hotel. _____ 114

Hotel Dining. _____ 119

Dining out. _____ 121

Calling home. _____ 123

Shopping duty free and customs. _____ 125

Your first purchases in a foreign country. _____ 133

5 ON THE TOUR _____ 138

The first day talk. _____ 138

The Tour Director. _____ 149

Getting along with people. _____ 151

What the tour involves. _____ 153

Complaints. _____ 162

Differences. _____ 167

Transport systems. _____ 174

Meeting the locals. _____ 178

Motorway service stops. How they work. _____ 179

Travel security. _____ 183

Pickpockets. _____ 185

Taking your photos. _____ 188

Tipping. _____ 191

Optional tours. _____ 201

A sample itinerary. _____ 224

What to do in case of an emergency. _____ 235

Precautionary measures that could save you thousands. _____ 239

6 **COMING HOME** _____ 243

The last couple of days. _____ 243

Keeping in touch. _____ 244

After the tour. _____ 245

7 **THINGS TO PHOTOCOPY** _____ 249

List of films used (4 rolls of 36 photos). _____ 250

Contact and address list. _____ 254

Contact and address list. _____ 255

Movies to watch to get you in the mood. _____ 256

EMERGENCY CONTACT LIST 'A'. _____ 258

EMERGENCY CONTACT LIST 'B'. _____ 259

DISCLAIMER:

PREFACE

So you want to do a coach tour of Europe and need more information. Look no further. Because I have worked in the coach touring industry for about sixteen years and have seen how various tour companies work. I have also listened to countless clients complain that they weren't able to access all the information required prior to their travel experience so I have decided to put pen to paper to remedy that situation.

The same questions arise time after time so if you are thinking of travelling, either by way of backpacking, or taking an escorted holiday, this book is a must read. It is also a valuable investment which will help you make a more informed decision about which holiday product is going to suit you best.

It will provide information that your travel agent possibly didn't have. And much other information of the type you never normally hear about until your holiday is actually under way.

We will discuss how to interpret brochures, i.e. the difference between seeing and visiting, and how to work out just what is and isn't included. We will also discuss safety and security, and how to get the most out of your holiday. We will highlight the many little things that can be done before your departure so that when your holiday commences you can sit back and relax and not worry about what is going on back home.

In short, this book will make you travel savvy and save you a considerable amount of money at the same time.

Bon voyage!

INTRODUCTION

I have always had it in mind to sit down and write a book designed to help people understand what the travel industry is all about. Such a book would not necessarily unravel all the mysteries of the industry but would at least materially assist those about to set out on journeys to foreign lands. Over the years I have found that many people arriving in a foreign country are not aware of what they are letting themselves in for so my book would need to contain information not necessarily available from time-strapped travel agents. Nor always available from people who have already been on a tour. Many of these travellers either misinterpret, or do not have enough facts, to properly explain to their friends what is really involved.

There are many modes of travel, and many different types of people wanting to travel. The important thing is to match the right person with the right product. As well as this there is a special balance to travelling which if not attained can result in a never-to-be-forgotten disaster instead of the hoped-for holiday of a lifetime.

One of the most important things to resolve before setting out on any holiday is to know what you want. How many days would you like to be away? What cities would you like to see? How long would you like to stay in each city? What standard of accommodation are you hoping for? If you do not make these decisions before approaching a travel agent you might find that browsing through numerous brochures, and the companies producing them, will cause endless confusion. You will probably be spoiled for choice.

The advantages of this book ....

- **It contains answers to questions you may never think to ask.**

- **It takes the time to tell you what you really need to know.**

- **Nothing else quite like it on the market.**

- **Printed in larger font for easier reading while on the road.**

HOW TO WRITE YOUR OWN TRAVEL JOURNAL

Included in this book is a series of pages designed to prompt your thoughts and give you the tools to help you write your own travel story. During my time as a tour director I found that about 20 to 30 percent of my clients always compiled a travel journal over the course of their tour. So with this in mind I have prepared a list of relevant points elsewhere in this book to assist those interested in this sort of thing. People are interested in this form of record and I strongly suggest doing so.

At an early stage you should check all the things that need doing before departing for overseas. And once under way, record your thoughts as you go. You will want to write down how your travel journey is progressing, and there will be times when you feel the task you've undertaken isn't so much fun after all. Especially when you start getting varying opinions from other people who have done tours, or people who know people who have done tours. Sometimes this information is conflicting, and the best way to handle it is to stop listening for awhile, sit back and relax with a cup of coffee, and remember what your own personal reason was for coming on the tour in the first place.

- Record a list of what to do and what not to do.

- Keep a record of day to day events. Assistance is given with the day by day tour planner.

- Information provided should include day number, wake-up call, breakfast details, bags-out time and departure time.

- List specific tasks for the day, i.e. change money, phone home, etc etc.

- List best memory for the day.

- List priceless moment for the day, i.e. something that could not be bought.

- List money spent for the day, i.e. money changing, coffee, impulse purchases.

- Commission shopping lunches. More often than not, when you realize just how much you are spending on your own you will begin to realize just what good value it is doing things together as a group.

1

TRAVEL IN GENERAL

What is travel?

Travel can be defined as stepping outside our normal boundaries. Or leaving our comfort zones to go to other lands to see for ourselves how other cultures operate. In the process we will experience history first hand. We will experience different art, different flavours, different foods, different styles and ways of doing things. And people who do this are to be commended.

It takes courage to leave comfort and security behind to travel to the other side of the world. People who do are throwing themselves into a completely new environment in the hope of gaining new knowledge or else building up a store of new experiences. For every person who does travel there are thousands who don't and these are the ones who remain at home waiting to hear all about it. There are certain sacrifices which must be made to turn holiday dreams into reality but the rewards of travel far outweigh them. Travel invigorates.

Travel renews. It gets us out of our rut and make new people of us. So in that sense travel could almost be described as a healing tonic.

Why do we travel?

- ## TO EXPERIENCE DIFFERENT CULTURES AND WAYS OF LIFE.

People travel for many different reasons. Whether for business or pleasure I always tell my groups that I feel very fortunate to work as a tour guide because I work in an industry which caters for people who are doing what they really want to. Unlike some of my doctor and dentist friends whose clients only come to them because they have to. So why is it then that we hear so many talk about how they would like things to be as they are back home when they know they are going to come up against something completely different?

There is an old saying that a tourist is someone who travels to a foreign land to experience all the things that don't exist back home and then sometimes has trouble adjusting to some of the differences they encounter. Things like differences in culture, alternative ways of life, different food, different art, and different history.

These differences are what make travelling so interesting. But even so, sometimes there are a few who spend most of their time complaining that things are not the way they thought they would be.

I want to share with you a story about one of my own travel experiences in Budapest, Hungary, which relates to the disproportionate amount of dog poo on the streets of Budapest.

When I first began to visit Budapest to visit my girlfriend who is a local city guide there I had a great trouble dealing with one of the cultural differences. Her old apartment was situated in one of the more densely populated parts of the city. Between her flat and the local market is a street referred to by both of us as the Dog Poo Street, where for some unknown reason most of the local dog owners are in the habit of bringing their dogs for one purpose only. With the result that the street has a unique perfume and is also a veritable minefield of dog poo. So much so that it is usually necessary to make a large detour around this street to get to the market. I became so obsessed with all the dog poo during my early days in the country that I found it hard to enjoy anything else the city had to offer for fear of treading in you-know-what.

Until one day, my girlfriend told me that after listening to all my complaints about the dogs and their dirty habits she wondered whether I had noticed any of the other attractions the city was noted for. Things like the Ballet Sparticus being performed at the National Opera Theatre, or enjoying dinner and the ambience of the city while looking out over the beautiful Danube at night with the illuminated palaces of Budapest and the old Hungarian Empire in the background, or being fascinated with the magnificent architecture of the beautiful chain bridge which joins the two cities of Buda and Pest. Although this shocked me at first I think she was trying to tell me that it was a question of getting my priorities right. And from that point on I began to see more beauty in both the country and the people of Hungary.

- ## TO BROADEN OUR HORIZONS AND CREATE NEW EXPERIENCES TO SHARE WITH OUR FAMILY AND FRIENDS.

One of the main reasons people choose to travel is to broaden their horizons and have new experiences to share with their family and friends when they return back home to their own countries. These experiences can range from sampling new types of cuisine to meeting and interacting with locals in their various countries. Or from purchasing a can of Coca Cola to observing different types of behaviour on the roads. Or from noting how local children attend school to finding out about the unusual phone and fax systems in some countries.

Something I do find however is that when people have had time to think about all these different things they quickly gain a new appreciation of customs and methods in the country they call home. And I have heard this said over the years that travel makes you appreciate you own home territory just that little bit more. Where we normally live is where we are most comfortable. However to gain true appreciation of differences to our home we must travel and experience.

- ## TO HAVE A BREAK FROM THE NORMAL ROUTINE AT HOME.

Sometimes in our normal day to day routine we may find ourselves getting stuck in a rut. Many people have told me over the years how lucky I am to be doing the job I do. However, it didn't come easy. For me to enter the travel industry I first had to leave a secure job and run the risk of not having an income for a while. As well as that I had to break from my friends and stop being so involved in their lives.

Travelling is not always easy, or more precisely, it is both easy and not so easy at the same time. Easy because anyone can make out a cheque to a travel agent, or put down a visa card to book their flight and accommodation. But it is not so easy to make the break from a normally busy schedule back home, which might include having to decline certain invitations from family and friends, and missing events and celebrations which are important. But don't despair. Unless the events are major one-off occasions they'll roll around again in a years' time.

So I suggest that setting a firm date for your travel, and sticking to it, is of the utmost importance. That way people will know where they are with you, and it will also accomplish two things. First, your friends will be able to plan their events around the time you are away. And secondly, by telling everyone what you are doing will make you more determined to follow things through.

- ## IN ORDER TO SAY YOU HAVE BEEN THERE AND DONE THAT.

This would have to be one of the best and most rewarding reasons to travel. There is a great deal of satisfaction to be had by visiting unusual places and their famous landmarks. Also, being able to talk about the feeling of being overwhelmed by such attractions as the Colloseum and its sheer size, or the goose bumps you got when you walked the same paths that famous emporers and Kings walked over 2,000 years ago. Their stories when told by a guide who did more than just read words from a book will bring everything to life for you.

- ## TO BE ABLE TO RELATE TRAVEL EXPERIENCES TO SOME OF OUR FRIENDS.

For every person who is fortunate enough to take a major holiday to the far reaches of the globe there are many others who will never undertake such a journey. Some don't travel for a variety of reasons but it doesn't mean they aren't interested. With the result they will want to hear your travel stories. And when you combine your tales with the accurate record set out in your travel journal, and photographs of yourself and friends with people you have met in other countries, you will have solid reminders to jog your memory for years after. This will bring a lot of joy to people who wish you to share your experiences with them.

- ## SOMETIMES BECAUSE WE FEEL WE HAVE TO.

Some people travel because they feel they have to and the pressure to do this may come from many different sources. It could be because all their friends have travelled and they feel left out of conversations about travel because they have no experiences to share. Or they are forced to travel at a time governed totally by work restraints. The demands of their employers or chosen field of work can often dictate when a holiday can be taken.

Whatever the reason, if you are travelling because you feel you have to it is a good idea to have a long, hard think about what you are about to do because why would you want to invest your hard earned money in something you are not sure about? As well as doing what is best for yourself you need also to consider the impact on the people you will meet while you are away. If you are not feeling positively happy about what you are doing then maybe you should put it off until you are ready. Or if you decide to go anyway then what you really need to do is say to yourself: O.K. Maybe this is not the perfect time to do this, but since it is the only time I can I should treat myself to something a little special. But most importantly, I must remember that the people I meet along the way are not going to want to hear me complain about the fact that I didn't really want to come.

Now having said all this, I have met many people over the years who have been reluctant travellers whether holidaying alone or in a group. But once these people got away and started to relax they soon became so captivated by the sights and sounds of the cities and the beautiful aromas of the magnificent food halls. They found that by relaxing and going with the flow they eventually reached the stage where they were unwilling for the holiday to end. So whatever problems you may encounter on the road – get over them and get on with having fun.

The types of people who generally travel.

Our travel friends can be light-heartedly classified under the following headings ...

- **THE PERSON WHO IS ALWAYS HAPPY.**

This is the person you will want to spend as much time as possible with while you are away. Good things always seem to happen to people like this. They are positive and carefree and always willing to help if something goes wrong. In fact they are the type of people who with some historical knowledge, a sense of humour, and good organizational skills would be very good in the role of the tour director.

- **THE PERSON WHO ALWAYS COMPLAINS.**

This is usually the person who has complained for most of their life about everything and nothing. Their complaints can begin on the first day of a tour and can be about the country they are in not being like their homeland, or the fact that they are constantly tired because they were unable to sleep well. They usually have a lot going on at work and shouldn't really be taking this holiday. They don't find the locals friendly, their bags were lost at the airport. It's too hot. It's too cold. Why are the major cities so far apart? Why doesn't anyone speak English? And so on and so on.

This type of person will generally try to bring other people around to their way of thinking, and will do whatever they can to find fault with all aspects of the travel industry. There is a saying that applies to these people – 'misery looks for friends'.

So if you encounter this person while travelling and they are looking for someone to agree with their complaints, try to sympathize with them but at the same time bring to their attention that not everything is such a disaster and it would be better if they were to enjoy their day because life is too short not to enjoy every minute of it. Oh, by the way. They will probably be telling everyone what a load of rubbish this statement is.

- **THE PERSON WHO ALWAYS COMPLAINS BUT DOESN'T KNOW WHY.**

As above, but with no substance.

- **THE PERSON WHO IS ALWAYS HAPPY BUT DOESN'T KNOW WHY.**

Once again a great person to be spending your time with as their positive vibes will flow onto you.

- **THE PERSON WHO DOESN'T EVEN KNOW WHAT THE HOLIDAY INVOLVES, I.E. THEIR PARTNER BOOKED IT, OR THEY WON IT AS A PRIZE.**

These people are great. Sometimes their partner has booked their holiday and did not really discuss what it involved. Sometimes this can be a good thing. And sometimes not so good. I have had people who didn't even know how many days their holiday was, or even what cities they were going to visit. Which is in very stark contrast to the person who wants to know more than the tour director. Sometimes there are people who have won the trip as a promotion – which is a great thing. However if you fall into this category one thing you should never do is complain about the price of anything as you may already be several thousand dollars ahead of your travelling companions due to your windfall and they will view you as ungrateful.

- **THE PERSON WHO HAD THE TOUR BOOKED BY A FRIEND.**

This is the person who may have been too busy to go to the travel agent, or just didn't know where to start when it came to travel. So they took the easy way out and let someone else take care of everything. Which is fine, unless of course they wanted to have a different travel experience to what they were having.

- THE PERSON WHO IS ONLY ON TOUR BECAUSE THEY FELT THEY HAD TO DO THE TRIP BECAUSE ALL THEIR FRIENDS HAD DONE IT.

Not always too happy about being on holiday but felt obliged to travel because all their friends had done so. They feel they are missing out on something by not being able to share their friends' experiences and therefore come away on holiday with a degree of reluctance.

- THE PERSON WHO THINKS THEY BOOKED A FIVE STAR ALL-INCLUSIVE HOLIDAY.

Sometimes this is an impression wrongly obtained from travel agents and well-meaning friends. Sometimes the holiday has been completely misrepresented and the client feels very upset with the product they are now receiving. If you should find these people on your tour it is generally best to empathize with them and suggest they put their case in writing straight away, along with the travel agent's details, and fax this immediately to the travel agent. As well as this, give a copy of the correspondence to the tour director soother she can pass this on directly to their company so the matter can be attended to.

By doing this straight away two things will be achieved ... First, the client will generally feel better knowing that their complaint is being attended to. And second, it will provide valuable information to the tour company as to the way their product is being represented by their agents.

- **THE PERSON WHO THOUGHT EVERYTHING WAS INCLUDED – INCLUDING SEVERAL THINGS NOT MENTIONED EVEN IN THE BROCHURE.**

This is a very rare bird and I have only come across this type of person once in my fourteen years on the road. On the particular tour I was conducting, it was necessary to allow my clients to participate in some optional excursions before having the opportunity to collect the payment for these. Due to the constraints of time I was not able to collect the money and get signed authorization from my clients until the third day of the tour. When this time came around one of my clients who was travelling as part of a party of four decided that he did not want to pay for the optional tours he had participated in because he felt he was led to believe the optional tours were included in the overall package.

This is quite interesting for several different reasons. Firstly he had obtained some of his information for the tour from the internet, and some by fax from their travel agent, being too busy to actually visit the agency in person.

Based on these two sources of partial information he chose his tour. But the optional ones he claimed he had been led to believe were included were not mentioned anywhere at all within his source material. So it was difficult for me to understand how he could believe they were included.

The real beauty of these clients was that even after stating they did not want to pay for the optionals which they had already availed themselves of they also felt they should be permitted to attend future optionals at no cost to them. Without going into too much detail, suffice it to say that the client just discussed did not conclude the tour.

- ## THE PERSON WHO ALWAYS KNOWS MORE THAN THE TOUR DIRECTOR.

The person who knows more than the tour director is actually quite an interesting individual because from time to time they can be quite helpful. And the tour director can often have interesting conversations with them. Unfortunately at other times they have this compulsion to let everyone else know that they are more clued up than the tour director. And they do go to a lot of trouble to acquire that knowledge. They sometimes go to the internet and download massive amounts of information about opening and closing times of various institutions and facilities, for example, and have pretty well done the tour director's job for him. The real question is why? Especially when the tour director could have told them pretty well everything they needed to know anyway.

I have even seen people like this placing notices on Company bulletin boards seeking details of which tour director would be on what tour and whether anyone could supply information about them. Whether they had been involved in bad incidents in the past. Whether they had a sound knowledge of the history of various locations, and so forth. But all this could easily turn out to be a fruitless activity for a number of reasons. Only one of them being, that the tour director being enquired about may get re-scheduled on to another tour at the last minute for any different number of reasons.

Advertising their own knowledge to the group and thrusting their knowledge forward **seems** to be a psychological necessity for these people. They don't often have a lot of social skills which tends to unfortunately make them somewhat incompatible with many people in the group.

- ## THE PERSON WHO WANTS TO BE THE TOUR DIRECTOR.

Once again this person only appears on tour from time to time, much to the tour director's delight. Hopefully, if and when they do appear you will have a tour director who is capable of working with them so that the tour will still run effectively. The type of person who generally wants to take control of the group will be a person with a strong character and this can either be a great benefit or act as a destructive influence. If the latter, they will want people to follow them and go against the advice of the tour director.

- ## THE PERSON WHO SHOULD HAVE BEEN THE TOUR DIRECTOR.

From time to time you may find that you have someone in the group who is very knowledgeable, friendly, and organized and would be quite capable of conducting the tour all by themselves. Hopefully your tour director will acknowledge this person's intelligence and ability, and this person will in return respect the fact that the tour director has a job to do.

- ## THE PERSON WHO DOES NOT CARE MUCH EITHER WAY.

What a delight to have this person on tour. They generally enjoy everything, they don't care what they see or do, and sometimes don't know what the itinerary is or what city they are going to visit next. They will willingly participate in all that is offered and be appreciative of all they are involved with. Be sure to spend some time with these people as you can find it will be time well spent.

- ## THE LEADER IN THE GROUP AND THE FOLLOWERS.

This person can be a combination of several different types of the abovementioned, and once again can be fun, or a total disaster waiting to happen should they be on your tour. On the positive side, they will insist that as many people as possible follow the advice of the tour director and participate as much as possible in order to get the maximum amount of enjoyment from being on a group tour. On the negative side, they will try to undermine the tour director's efforts to get everyone involved in various outings. They will try to convince their fellow travellers that rather than follow the advice of the tour director they would be better off listening to what they have to say. That way they will have a better time and see more of the real side of travel. Ignoring the tour leader will mean better shopping, and money-changing deals, better information on tipping or anything else that involves financial transactions. And they will make all sorts of guarantees as to the validity and reliability of their information upon which you should be prepared to base the future enjoyment of your holiday. At first this person will seem like a real life-saver to the traveller who has probably already heard the horror stories of group travel and tour company rip offs.

But a cautionary note about these people. I would suggest that you ask them a question or two beginning with – 'what's in it for them?' Secondly, ask them what guarantee they can give that all the things they are telling you will actually happen.

I mention this because so many times I have seen people leave a city or a country disappointed because someone on tour made a whole lot of big promises which turned out to be hollow. These people had chosen to follow the wrong advice only to find that upon arriving in a major city such as Rome or Paris the person who had made all the promises of showing them a great time had decided now that they wanted to do their own thing, which meant that their new friends who had put their faith in them were now effectively abandoned. And unfortunately, at such late notice, it was then not possible for them to join in with what the group was doing. And they ended up not leaving the hotel because it was all just too much effort.

Now I know that some people reading this will say – 'that would not happen to us because even if the original plans fell apart we would still get out on our own and discover the city'. However what people do not take into account are all the variables which are discussed in depth in the 'optional tour' section. These might include such things as local transport strikes, local taxi strikes, hotel book-outs, and closures out of the control of your tour operator.

So why do these people want you to be their friend? Why would they want to spend their holiday doing for free what the tour director is being paid for? And if they have such an anti tour group mentality why did they come on such a tour in the first place?

Now the interesting thing about this is the fact that as they go about suggesting more and more people join in with them, and more and more listen, they will in effect be creating a new group. And the point of being an individual then disappears. Because you then have a number of individual people trying to navigate the city on public transport on which there can be separations. Or taxis ending up at different venues despite all being given the same address. And as well as these complications, at the end of the evening when trying to divide the bill, it is not unusual for a thirty minute debate to ensue over who ate and drank what, and what it cost, and what does the bill mean by a 'bread and butter charge', and who can understand the 'local tax charge' and so forth. And no matter how good or bad the service might have been you still have to pay a gratuity because you were a small group, etc, etc.

So once again, if you are going to follow this type of persons recommendation, and they are going to give you the same guarantees that your tour director offers you to resolve any problems that may arise, you have to ask yourself what is in it for them.

Generally, the reason these people do what they do is because they have not prepared themselves properly for the type of tour they have booked. Rather than spend the extra money to enjoy the experiences being offered by a professional company with an established reputation they choose to try to bring people down to their level so they will have someone to spend their time with.

Their real motive is not your enjoyment, but theirs.

So why did they come on holiday? A lot of the time I have no idea why these people choose to come on a group tour.

The different ways to travel.

In this section we are going to look at a comparison between the various methods of travelling, and to retain balance, will look at both the advantages and disadvantages of each. You will then be able to choose for yourself which method suits you best.

- **'I WANT TO BE INDEPENDENT', WE IN THE TRAVEL INDUSTRY HEAR PEOPLE CRY. BUT WHAT DOES IT REALLY MEAN?**

Well it means exactly that. It means you are on your own. Free, because you do not belong to anyone. Autonomous and self-governing, meaning you do not have to answer to anyone. When on your own you are completely responsible for solving and dealing with whatever situation may and will arise while you are enjoying this form of independence. You must find your own way when seeking directions and decide whether the information you have been given is accurate or not.

This can be a good thing if you have no particular itinerary or agenda and do not really care what lies ahead, and it suited me when I first began to travel. However my first independent travel experiences took place in my home country Australia at a time in the mid-1980's when things were quite simple and relaxed. People I met along the way were friendly and helpful and not as wary of strangers as many seem to be today. So there were a lot of things going in my favour.

I would still recommend this form of travel for some people but suggest that you try it out in your own country first for a few days just to get the feel of it. Go to a city which appeals to you and experience something completely new. Go with nothing pre-booked so that you have the freedom to choose once you arrive.

I believe this will give you a good idea of the costs involved and the various kinds of experience you can have in the world of independent travel.

Good luck, and have fun.

- ## HERE ARE THE PLUSSES AND MINUSES OF TRAVELLING ON YOUR OWN.

ADVANTAGES:

1 You answer to no one.
2 You work out your own agenda.
3 You have the opportunity to meet many different types of people.
4 You are as free as a bird.

DISADVANTAGES:

1 You get no special or significant discounts as you are not a significant number of people.
2 You generally pay full price for everything.
3 You can end up getting lonely and even bored.
4 You'll have no one to help you when things go wrong.
5 You are responsible for everything.
6 You must make the agenda.
7 You could meet any type of person.
8 You don't get information given to you which has already been filtered.
9 You can and will spend a lot of time researching and planning your days when there are specific things you need to see.
10 There are no guarantees that the information you will be given is correct or accurate.

11 When things go wrong – and they will – that is the time you will fully realize what doing it on your own is all about.

12 You will not get to see as much as if someone co-ordinated your trip for you.

• HIRING A CAR. WHAT DOES IT INVOLVE, AND WHAT ARE THE COSTS?

ADVANTAGES:

1 You choose your mode of transport.
2 You are able to get away from the main roads.
3 You can set your own timetable.
4 You gain a great feeling of independence doing it on your own.
5 You can stay as long or short a time as you like.
6 You have more opportunities to see the small towns.

DISADVANTAGES:

1 You can spend a lot of time worrying about where to legally park.
2 You will have trouble in large cities with parking and traffic and dealing with aggressive drivers and different road laws.
3 Only one person gets to see the countryside. The other gets to see the roads.
4 Having to adapt to the different driving etiquette of each country.

5   Having to learn the different road laws of the countries you wish to visit.

6   Difficult to calculate the amount of time required between each point and to know the best times to arrive and depart from the various points on interest.

7   You can waste time getting lost on small roads because signposting is unfamiliar.

COSTS:

1   Calling and booking the car.

2   Cost of getting to and from the point of pick up and drop off for the vehicle to be hired.

3   Fuel in Europe at the time of writing was approximately 1 euro per litre or 6 U.S. dollars per gallon.

4   Parking the car each night at the hotel can cost approximately 10 euro per night.

5   Cost of parking the vehicle during the day when sightseeing depends on location. However often it can be difficult to understand the different regulations and whether or not your vehicle will be legally parked in the area you choose. Many European countries especially in city areas, will either clamp the wheels of the illegally parked vehicle or they will simply tow it away to a compound where it can be collected once the fine is paid. This can be approximately 130 euro for a wheel clamp release and up to 300 euro for retrieving the vehicle from the compound.

6   Toll charges for the use of motorways and major road systems vary greatly from country to country. Some

countries such as France, Spain and Italy will charge on the basis of distance driven by having toll stations located at various points along the way. The most common method of payment is by cash. Many of the toll stations will advertise a credit card service but these aren't always reliable. Other countries such as Hungary and Austria set a flat fee for a set amount of days you wish to use the road. For example in Hungary you pay approximately 8 euro for a ten day permit to use the motorway. Austria also operates on a similar system. In these countries you are well advised to purchase the correct stickers or permits required as strong policing in this matter means that not knowing the law isn't tolerated as an excuse. The stickers are known as 'vignettes' and can be purchased at the fuel station prior to entering the country where the permit is required. Or at the customs/border point, or the first fuel station upon entering the new country. Unless of course you are going to Switzerland in which case the border guards will supply you with the correct permit upon arrival into their country for approximately 20 euro for two days.

7   The cost of hiring the vehicle could run to 50 euro per day.

8   To help with your calculations I would suggest you allow fuel and toll costs at about 160 euro for each 600kms/or 400 miles you plan to drive.

9   So a summary of these costs would run something like this. If you were to visit seven cities in six different countries over a period of fifteen days,

driving approximately 3200kms or 2000 miles, parking the vehicle in hotel carparks you could spend approximately 1800 euro for this part of your holiday. Remembering however, that for the poor driver it won't really seem like a holiday for them unless of course they love driving.

- ## FLYING BETWEEN CITIES.

ADVANTAGES:

1 Definitely the quickest form of transport. Over great distances.
2 Ability to earn frequent flyer points.
3 Opportunity to see more distant places in a shorter period of time.

DISADVANTAGES:

1 Flying is usually very expensive.
2 Can be complicated to organize if more than a couple of people.
3 Tiring due to jet lag and atmospheric changes.
4 You see nothing of the countryside.
5 It can be claustrophobic shut up in a plane.

COSTS:

When choosing flying between cities as your main form of travel some of the things to take into consideration are as follows…

1 Travel times to and from the airport can vary considerably depending on the location of your accommodation. However I have found that when moving between cities by almost any form of transport a whole day needs to be set aside because there are many procedures now in place which tend to further delay what is in reality the luxury of air travel over relatively short distances. So much so that in many European cities airlines have opted to use high speed rail connection between airports as opposed to plane connections. For example in London you can arrive at Waterloo Station just forty five minutes before the departure of the Eurostar, board the train which takes three hours to arrive at a central Paris rail station, as opposed to travelling up to forty five minutes to London's Heathrow Airport, followed by a one hour check in and then a one hour flight to Charles de Gaulle airport north of the city. Then to get to the centre of Paris further transport is required.

2 If you add the two methods of transport times together you can see that there is not too much difference but for convenience, most people would prefer to utilize the method with the minimum amount of connections required. Especially when the price differential is minimal.

3 Also to consider when allowing time for checking in at international terminals is that approximately up to three hours is required for the purpose, as opposed to about one hour at domestic terminals.

4   The main disadvantage with air travel is the expense. There are such things as discounted fares but these can often be unappealing for other reasons. You may be lumbered with terrible schedules such as the very first or very last flights of the day as well as zero flexibility and very limited availability.

5   I would only recommend intercity travel by air nowadays in the following circumstances. Where the distance needed to travel is greater than 600 kilometres (or 400 miles) and there is no high speed rail service between the cities.

- **GOING BY EURORAIL**

ADVANTAGES:

1   You get to see the countryside.
2   Some train journeys are spectacular.
3   You can go for a walk around.
4   Can be quite fast.
5   You get to meet some interesting people from many different countries.

DISADVANTAGES:

1   No direct information given to you.
2   You are on your own to resource all information.
3   You must be vigilant when it comes to security.
4   You may miss your stop if you cannot understand the announcements in the local language.
5   You waste a lot of time continually moving between your accommodation and the rail station.

6   Sometimes the queues for a taxi in major cities can be horrendous.
7   Not so economical when you add in accommodation and additional transport.
8   Vulnerable to theft if you fall asleep in a general sit-up compartment.

COSTS:

1   For a Eurorail pass which covers the main seventeen European countries the price ranges from fifteen consecutive days travel for approximately 600 euro up to three months consecutive travel for approximately 1700 euro. This works out at approximately 18 to 40 euro per day if you use it every day.
2   For periods where you can pick and choose your travel days over a specified period you will pay approximately 730 euro for ten days travel over a two month period, or approximately 930 euro for fifteen days travel within a two month period.
3   Something to consider with the above passes is that you may need to pay an additional booking fee if you do not want to take pot luck when you arrive at the train station and would prefer the security of a reservation.
4   Purchasing maps.
5   Cost of getting to and from your accommodation each time you move cities.
6   Food can be very expensive and there may be little choice when it comes to lunches and snacks. This is

because the one and only shop on the train, i.e. no competition.

7 You may wish to check the following websites for more information ...
Rail Europe: www.raileurope.com
Eurorail: www.eurorail.com

- ## DOING A COACH TOUR.

ADVANTAGES:

1 You benefit from the purchasing power of the group.
2 Easy to budget for if you have been correctly informed.
3 You will get to see and experience more than you could possibly imagine in the time available.
4 You can enjoy the local wines and beers and not have to worry about driving.
5 Accompanied by a tour director or local guide at most points so should any situations arise you will have the services of a person with local knowledge and contacts to help you overcome any obstacles.
6 Tour co-ordinated for you as much or as little as you require.
7 You will be in the company of like-minded people. All you need to do is relax and enjoy yourself.
8 Most relevant information given to you at the time. No need to fish through books to find what you want.
9 Information generally given on the history, geography, industries, cultural and social aspects as well as any further relevant information on the

countries travelled to will be given by your tour director or local guides where used.

10 Greatest possibility of up to date information. Unfortunately, many guide books will be out of date by the time they are printed. For example, opening and closing times of museums and restaurants, as well as the fact that they cannot predict, major conference dates in the larger capitals where and when you may be booked in to stay. So it will be impossible to get a booking at a good venue or cabaret if you don't already have one. A good example of this was that I was told if I went to Las Vegas between Monday and Thursday I would get a good rate on a hotel as this was the off period for the city. However when I arrived I was told that there was a worldwide electronics convention being held, and whereas on a normal Thursday I could have stayed at a luxury hotel for around 150 U.S. dollars a night, the demand for accommodation on this particular Thursday was so high I would have to pay the full rate of 600 U.S. dollars if I wanted a room. I tried several hotels and the same situation applied so I had to drive to another town in order to get a room within my budget.

DISADVANTAGES:

1 You need to choose your itinerary in advance.
2 You have to relax and go with the flow.

COSTS:

1   Initial cost of the tour
2   Optional excursions.
3   Meals not covered by either of the above.

- **CYCLING**

This is the perfect way to get a real taste for what a country has to offer in a specific region. Most people who choose this method will travel approximately 50 km per day and spend between seven to fourteen days on this type of holiday. If this is your chosen method of travel be sure to have a medical check before departing your own country. It is a good idea to be at a reasonable level of fitness before you depart.

ADVANTAGES:

1   Can be very cheap.
2   Good for your health as long as you don't get knocked over.
3   You get a real feel for the country you travel.
4   You can stop wherever you want.
5   A good chance to meet the locals.

DISADVANTAGES:

1   You should have a mechanical knowledge of bikes.
2   You may get a feel for the country literally if you get knocked over.
3   You must travel very light.

4   You are on your own.
5   You may get lost and waste a lot of time.
6   Difficult to co-ordinate time.
7   You can only see a small part of a lot of territory.
8   Drinking and riding not allowed.
9   You must be very aware of bad drivers.
10 Adverse weather conditions may ruin the holiday.

COSTS:

1   Bike hire.
2   Purchasing of spare you may not use.
3   All meals.
4   Accommodation.
5   Safety gear must be hired or purchased.
6   Maps.
7   Guide books.
8   Purchase of suitable clothing including wet weather gear.

- **HITCH-HIKING OR BACKPACKING:**

When I was back-packing I had many things stolen, particularly at hostels which can sometimes be frequented by unsavoury types who make a living out of preying on travellers.

ADVANTAGES:

1   A great deal of freedom.
2   No need to plan an itinerary.
3   You never know where you are going to end up and sometimes this can be a lot of fun.

4   Inexpensive if you stay out of the main cities.
5   You can meet a lot of very interesting people.

DISADVANTAGES:

1   Can be a little dangerous if the wrong people pick you up.
2   Can be lonely.
3   You sometimes miss so much.
4   Can be very time consuming waiting for lifts.
5   Can be expensive if you don't have accommodation booked and you need to stay in a hotel.   In many places free camping is forbidden.
6   Security risks at hostels.

COSTS:

1   Accommodation.
2   Food.
3   Backpack.
4   Sleeping bag.
5   Suitable equipment, i.e. wet-weather gear, good set of boots, etc.
6   Security items such as wire cages built to wrap around packs, back-pack locks, personal and portable alarm systems.

• WALKING

It is possible to save a lot of money by walking between cities but this method does use up a lot of time.

ADVANTAGES:

1   Keeps you fit.
2   Some people actually make a living out of this. They are able to obtain sponsorships from various companies to do walks of up to several hundred kilometres at a time. Eventually a few get to see much of the world in this way.

DISADVANTAGES:

1   Can take you forever.
2   Only for the seriously fit.
3   Incredible discipline required.

COSTS:

As for hitch-hiking, but add more for blister relief.

• BEGGING

I have actually met people who financed their way around the world by asking other people for money as they went along. Sometimes this works well. Sometimes it doesn't. The different responses encountered are as different as people are different. Some have been very generous with beggars, donating them several hundred dollars with the only condition being that the traveller contacts them later to report of their progress.

ADVANTAGES:

1   Shouldn't cost you anything at all.
2   You get to meet lots of interesting people.

DISADVANTAGES:

1   You have no idea whether or not anyone is going to give you any money.
2   Can be a little bit humiliating.
3   Some people will look down on you and shun you from their society.

Different times to travel.

- JANUARY/FEBRUARY:

Travelling in January and February can be both beautiful and rewarding. Beautiful because of the different vistas that open up in winter, and rewarding because the resorts are much less crowded.

The snow-covered mountains are busy with cross-country and downhill skiers all looking for the next perfect run. Beautiful panoramas of valleys with small typical villages nestled in amongst the rises and falls of the terrain. And trees who's leaves which were golden orange in autumn have now been replaced with a dusting of snow sitting atop the dark chocolate branches and twigs like icing on the fingers of the richest of chocolate cakes.

Combine all this with the changes of menu from summer to winter in many of the countries and you have a fascinating mix of sights, sounds and fragrances which even if you have travelled around Europe before in summer will make you feel you are seeing the continent for the first time.

However in order to really enjoy Europe in winter be sure to read the section on winter travel and the importance of the proper clothing for this time of the year. If you do this I am quite sure you will have a great time.

- EASTER

The Easter holiday break can result in large volumes of traffic on the roads. Even in a well organized and relatively polite traffic country such as England I would sometimes stay home at Easter watching the massive queues of traffic up to twenty miles in length and traffic jams lasting for three, four, or even five hours as people began their four day break on the M3 which heads south-west out of London in the direction of many of the lovely coastal towns and resorts in the direction of Southampton and Bournemouth. Nearby are the historic areas of Salisbury and Stonehenge. So if you choose to travel over the Easter period be prepared for some facilities not to be operational, and for the roads to be heavily congested.

• WHEN IS IT HOTTEST?

Europe's hottest months tend to be July and August and the following table gives an idea of average temperatures during this period ...

Paris	18C/64F	Budapest	21.5C/70F
Madrid	25C/77F	Prague	19.4C/67F
Florence	25C/77F	Berlin	19C/66F
Rome	25C/77F	Switzerland	18.5C/65F
Athens	28C/83F	Amsterdam	16.5C/62F
Cairo	28C/83F	Copenhagen	17C/63F
Vienna	20C/68F	Moscow	18.3C/65F

Some of these temperatures may not look too bad to many people however do understand that in recent years many of the major European cities have been experiencing days where the temperatures have climbed well into the high thirty degrees Celsius (or 100 degrees Fahrenheit or more).

I have escorted many groups through Europe at these times and the people have enjoyed themselves greatly. However to give a more accurate basis for comparison I will now set out a few average summer temperatures for some of your own countries ...

Alice Springs, Central Australia	28C/84F
Singapore	25.5C/78F
Bloemfontein, South Africa	23C/73F
Vancouver Canada	18C/73F
New Delhi India	31C/88F
Florida, USA	29C/84F

So if you do not travel well in the warmer months in your own country choose the cooler months to travel to Europe. And if you want to avoid the winter months there, i.e. December, January and February, this only leaves March to June and September to November as your best times to go. But remember to take into account daylight saving.

• EUROPEAN HOLIDAYS

The European holiday season will begin anywhere from around the first of July until the middle of August, depending on which country you are in.

This tends to be the warmest time of the year and is the reason why many Europeans head south to the various coastal resorts on Saturdays in particular, because Saturdays are changeover days. Most accommodation houses at the resorts offer packages that involve checking in on Saturday afternoons, staying seven nights, and then checking out on the following Saturday morning. New tenants check in on Saturday afternoon and the cycle starts all over again. Because of this custom traffic conditions throughout Europe are horrendous with all the holiday makers toing and froing on Saturdays. So be aware of all this if you are travelling in Europe from the 1st of July to the middle of August on a Saturday. Be prepared also for very crowded service stops en route.

- **CHRISTMAS AND NEW YEAR.**

Christmas celebrations for Europeans are most likely to take place on the evening of the 24th of December. Christmas Day itself being reserved for spending time with the family.

New Year is another matter. You need to remember that this is the dead of winter and if you are not conditioned to the cold or not wearing suitable clothing chances are you may not really enjoy yourself. Most celebrations are indoors and for this reason all suitable venues soon become crowded with patrons. People want to keep warm and be with other revellers as the midnight hour approaches.

However many venues will take advantage of the situation and charge premiums to enter their premises. Some may charge up to four time their normal fee, reacting to the old law of supply and demand. And people in search of fun and a quality experience seem prepared to pay the extra.

If you are on tour and wish to take part in New Year celebrations I very strongly recommend that you follow the advice of the tour director as they will want you to have the best night possible.

Travel Philosophy: *We all saved our money to come on holiday. We did not come on holiday to save our money.*

Many people while travelling seem to get caught up in worrying about the price of things too much. The reality is that wherever they choose to travel the price is the price and that's all there is to it. There's no point getting upset about the price of a drink, or the food you eat, because even on holiday you still have to drink and eat. Some people who choose to travel, continually worry about the money it's costing them and never get the chance to really enjoy what their holiday is all about.

Now realistically, by the time people have finished reading this book, they'll be more than adequately prepared to take a proper holiday. After a good read, and if they've taken note of some of the advice offered, they should find that being overly money-conscious won't be a problem.

• LET THE PROFESSIONALS DO THEIR JOB.

There's always a cheaper way to do things as we've already read earlier, i.e. you can walk, you can back-pack and you can hitch-hike. But by the same token it depends on what quality and what style of holiday you are looking for.

It's a bit like an operation. There's always a cheaper way to do it. Say one day you decide you need a tooth pulled out, and decide the cheapest way is to do it yourself, it may seem cheaper however this isn't an ideal thing to do. It's much better to pay a surgeon for their experience and know-how.

It is the same with the tour companies. They are the professionals when it comes to efficient holiday making. They have all the necessary knowledge to guide you in the best way to spend your travelling dollar or euro.

Ignoring the professionals is also a bit like people who try to fix their own plumbing. In order to save money and eliminate what they perceive to be the excessive charges of a registered plumber they go down to the hardware shop themselves and buy a wrench, and jointers, and nuts, etc, and head off back home. But on getting stuck in they overlook an intricate detail a plumbing expert may have picked up on. They strip a thread, there is a fountain of water inside the cupboard, and they are forced into the situation of having to call in the plumber anyway to fix the mess.

Something like this could end up costing the do-it-yourselfer double because the professional has to spend valuable time sorting out your mess first before they can fix anything else.

I'm a great believer in getting hold of qualified people first time to do the job properly. And when you do use a professional like this you usually end up getting a warranty or some kind of back-up in the unlikely event that something does go wrong in the future. So the idea is – do it once, do it right.

I went to a lawyer once who charged $400 an hour and a friend said to me 'gosh, I can get a lawyer much cheaper that that.' I explained to him that I could get a lawyer much cheaper than that too. I could get one for $100 an hour but unfortunately this chap was going to take six hours to solve my problem whereas the man charging $400 undertook to do the same task in one hour.

So let the professionals do their job. Sit back and relax. Let them look after you and have a great time because after all, we all have our own skills. You may be a professional in one area but perhaps not so professional in negotiating the European, or any other tourist circuit.

Homesickness; how to minimize and prevent it.

When you go on an extended holiday take some photos of your family and home with you. These help you cope with any homesickness which might arise and will also give your fellow travellers a chance to see where you come from and what you left behind.

Try not to make a rash decision to leave the trip part-way through and return home.

A lot of the time the homesickness can be related to culture shock. When you go away it is very exciting at first to see all the differences to what goes on back in your own country.

However sometimes you can feel quite overwhelmed and frustrated when you need to achieve a specific task, and realize that it is quite complicated due to the fact that you cannot speak the language and therefore cannot achieve what you would like to do.

This is when people miss home the most because they begin thinking about what is comfortable there and familiar. They miss the feeling of being able to have greater control of the environment around them and for this reason begin to focus on how much better and easier it would be back in their own environment where the surroundings are more comfortable.

If you ever feel this way on holiday I always suggest that it is a good idea at such times to take it easy and spend the day doing something which isn't demanding or taxing on you such as going to a café or reading a book.

What you also need to do is think back on how hard you worked and saved for this trip, and if you were to toss it in now, when would you be likely to return?

I have found that once many people begin to analyze their situation a little closer, and begin to share their homesick concerns with others, they get a lot of support from their fellow travellers and begin to forget about their homesick woes. They will decide to continue with their journey and start remembering that the purpose of coming on holiday in the first place was to have fun.

So if suffering from pangs of homesickness don't be embarrassed about telling others how you feel because you will find you will get a lot of support and encouragement from those around you to the extent that you will want to carry on. Don't suffer in silence.

2

PICKING A PRODUCT

The cost of a tour and where does the money go.

When you look into the cost of a tour as quoted by a travel agent there are many different factors to take into account.   Such things as the cost of producing the brochures and the agent's commission before departure. And then when the tour gets underway there are all the costs associated with hiring the coach, paying the driver, hotel accommodation, meals, the services of local guides and tour directors, porters, toll costs for use of motorways, parking of coaches, which can be up to 50 euro a day, or in extreme cases such as Florence a charge of approximately 200 euro per day is made for the coach just to enter the city. These days many other European cities are following this lead. Ferry crossings have to be paid for too. So when all these factors are added together it soon becomes apparent that a coach tour is excellent value for money.

- ## CONFUSING THE COST OF THE HOLIDAY WITH THE COST OF THE TOUR.

A very familiar comment I have heard over the years is from people discussing what their tour has cost them. From time to time I would hear some very large sums mentioned which just could not have been possible so this section is devoted to explaining separate costs and when measuring up value for money how you should really look at price versus value.

The cost of your tour is the cost **from** the point of departure. That city is the starting point. For example, if you book a tour where the departure point is London the cost will generally not include accommodation before or after the tour unless specified. The reason for this is that there may be people from London going on the tour.

So if you tour is twenty days long and costs 1600 euro then the average cost is 80 euro per day. So when you want to see if you've gotten value for money you have to ask yourself the following. If you were given eighty euro each morning of the tour – could you achieve the same benefits provided on the tour? Could you purchase your own sightseeing, travel-included dinners, breakfasts and so on for any less , travelling in the same level of comfort? Probably not.

When you look at the cost of your tour you should not include amounts such as travel to and from the departure city, accommodation before and after the tour, holiday travel insurance, or general day to day expenses such as coffee, snacks, rolls of film or shopping purchases. I firmly believe that once you have read this book fully, and used the information herein to choose and plan your trip, you will be as fully prepared as possible to have a hassle-free holiday. And definitely better prepared than anyone who has not read this book.

- **FLIGHTS AND ACCOMMODATION BEFORE AND AFTER THE TOUR.**

Many people don't take these costs into consideration believing them to be built in to the overall cost of the tour. Which they are not – unless the tour has been booked in the United States where it is part of their policy that these costs should be included. Depending on where the tour is starting or finishing, you can usually count on 150 euro per night for accommodation, not necessarily including breakfast.

- **TRAVEL INSURANCE AND WHAT IT INVOLVES.**

Travel insurance is usually sold at a bit of a premium but many see it as an essential thing to arrange before setting out. Not only are some policies handsomely priced, they don't always offer the cover you may need so it is a good idea to shop around with various travel agencies and insurance brokers.

Some people choose to enquire about travel insurance from their own home insurance companies, particularly when planning an extended tour overseas, because here they may be able to negotiate some kind of a rebate on any existing policies. For example, there is no point paying for three months of medical insurance in your own country if you are not going to be in your own country. Some companies might be willing to work around this by offsetting surplus premiums against a travel insurance.

- **TRANSFERS TO AND FROM THE AIRPORT.**

The cost of getting from your own home to the closest airport is something which shouldn't be overlooked. It's always worth checking on the internet about shuttle services at the various airports you'll find yourself at from time to time because most airports do have shuttle and taxi services.

If there are more than two or three of you travelling together it is sometimes quicker to use the local taxi service. A shuttle may be cheaper but it could have several drop-offs to make before finally reaching your hotel and the time involved could be considerable.

Coach touring and what are the differences.

- **COACHES, AND WHAT YOU GET FOR YOUR MONEY.**

The standard European coach is approximately twelve metres long, and on a budget coach or cost-saving tour will generally be fitted with up to fifty three seats. The pitch will not be exactly the same in each seat as these are installed manually and therefore some will have more room than others. For this reason it is a good idea to look for a company which offers a seat rotation policy so you are not susceptible to someone monopolizing the best seats for the entire tour.

- ## CLOSED AGE GROUP AND OPEN AGE GROUP TOURS. WHAT ARE THE DIFFERENCES?

Some tour companies operate tours which cater specifically for particular age groups. For example, Contiki run tours mainly for eighteen to thirty five year olds. Some tours are also put on for younger and older age groups, although on each of these specialist tours strays sometimes manage to latch on to a group to which they don't really belong. This is often done unwittingly , either because the travel agent didn't explain the requirement, or else the traveller wasn't paying attention when he/she was told the tour age restrictions and sometimes people know they are outside the restrictions however still try to participate anyway. If a stray is discovered at the point of departure it will be up to the discretion of the tour company whether or not the person is allowed to continue with the tour.

An open age group tour is as the name suggests. It is open to people of all ages right down to children as young as six or seven years old. On some of my tours I have had people up to eighty and eighty five years old who have been quite capable and fit on a tour and who enjoyed themselves immensely. A lot were fitter than people half their age. It was amazing to see these senior people getting up each morning with a sparkle in their eye, and rearing to go, while many of their much younger fellow travellers were crying out for more sleep.

If you are considering taking an open age group tour be prepared for a lot of fun. Particularly if there are children present. They can add a certain lightness to the proceedings and most people are happy to have them along.

• BUDGET TOURING

Some companies offer this style of tour for those on a limited budget. It is what could be called a 'skeleton' tour because most of the frills are lacking. For example, not every night is spent in a hotel. Accommodation is sometimes used in convents and monasteries, or else camping ground cabins. Such tours are usually escorted by a person from the country of departure whose knowledge is passed on to the tourists who are then sent out in ones and twos to see the sights unescorted. I have run into a number of people who have chosen this style of touring and something I did find quite interesting is that by the time you added up all the money they had been spending on their own, their costs were on a par with those people on an escorted tour.

This kind of touring suits some people, and they do enjoy it, but it requires a basic level of knowledge about the areas being entered, and a certain amount of self-reliance.

• COST-SAVING TOURS

These are tours which generally offer similar itineraries to both the closed group and the upper class tours the main difference being that the focus is on the sightseeing aspect of the tour. The cost is more or less for the bones or basics of the holiday and will include a simple style of accommodation in a combination of three and four star hotels, e.g. Ibis Mercure or Novotel hotels. These are usually several kilometres from the centre of town and offer basic clean comfortable and secure facilities.

All of the above is not such a bad thing however because by keeping the accommodation basic, clean and simple it also keeps the cost of the tour down and as mentioned, the primary focus of this kind of tour is to see many things in a limited period of time.

Sightseeing tours in major cities are often available with the help of local guides and vary greatly in length from one hour to three hours, yet will be enough to give a good taste of what the city has to offer. Included meals are also quite simple with breakfast being of continental nature, i.e. cereal, tea, coffee and maybe toast and juice. At many hotels it may be possible to upgrade your breakfast by paying a supplement.

The average age of clients on a tour like this will be around fifty five years old.

• UPPER FIRST CLASS

These tours make use of four and five star hotels and better. Coaches are fitted out with forty to forty nine seats for more room and substantial buffet breakfasts are the norm. There are all sorts of buffets which vary greatly from place to place. In some countries they may consist of bacon, sausages, eggs, cereals, fruits, yoghurts, omelets, hams and cheese, whereas in some other countries a buffet may be much simpler and lighter. Cereals, fruits, and occasionally ham, cheeses, salami, and different kinds of salad (e.g. Russian, cucumber and tomato, etc). In other cases breakfasts can often be so elaborate that they are more like lunch but are not necessarily composed of foods you are more familiar with in your own country. Although some establishments do make an effort to supply foods better known to the various tourists they are likely to encounter from time to time.

Examples of companies and their websites which offer the abovementioned variety of tours are as follows:

- www.trafalgartours.com
- www.insightvacations.com
- www.contiki.com
- www.globusandcosmos.com

• FIRST CLASS LUXURY

This is the next step up from upper first class yet only a tiny percentage of the travelling public makes use of tours of this kind. As the name implies they are characterized by a modest level of luxury based on an average cost of 250 to 300 euro per day. Although sometimes, this can reach 500 euro per day. The tours are pitched at the top end of the market and often there are only about sixteen to thirty five people in each touring party.

Some of the best hotels are used in each city and day by day such things as full buffet breakfasts, other meals, sometimes drinks, and tips are included as well.

People who use this type of tour usually expect the best and quite often, money is no object to them.

Some of the companies who provide First Class Luxury Tours are listed below. They don't advertise extensively and rely heavily on word-of-mouth recommendations from previously satisfied clients.

- Eurovista holidays in Europe.
  www.eurovistahols.com
- Tauck tours in Europe.
  www.tauck.com
- Abercrombie and Kent in Europe.
  www.abercrombiekent.com
- The Blue Train in South Africa.
  www.bluetrain.co.za
- Rocky Mountaineer Railways in Canada.
  www.rockymountaineer.com

Choosing the right tour.

When people are contemplating a tour they will generally go to a travel agent and ask for brochures. Sometimes the agent will thrust half a dozen on the counter and send the prospective client away with the words: 'have a look through these and when you find something you like come back and let me know'.

But this can soon become quite confusing. There are so many possibilities on offer, and they all look so exciting, and they're made to sound so enticing by the travel companies – which is fair enough – it's all part of modern marketing – that all of a sudden you find yourself with dozens and dozens of different tours to choose from and all are exciting and fun and look fantastic. You don't really know what to do.

- **BEFORE YOU EVEN SPEAK TO A TRAVEL AGENT.**

Before even speaking to a travel agent it is worth taking the time to sit down and work out a few things, i.e. you need to work out a strategy which enables you to choose the tour which suits your needs best. A strategy which will save you from being distracted by the hundreds of tours on offer and one which will enable you to narrow down very quickly a tour which is within your budget.

For example it is important to know how long you can spare for your holiday within the constraints of your occupation. How long you can be absent before everything will begin to fall apart at work. On the matter of time don't forget also to allow plenty to reach the departure point of the tour, and later, to return from it. It is better to arrive two or three days early at your departure point not only to shake off jet lag but also to allow yourself to adjust to a different season as well as a different time zone. There won't be time for these things once the tour begins.

Having sorted the time issue, compile a list of sights you know about and sights you would like to see.

• LISTING THE SIGHTS YOU ALREADY KNOW.

Thanks to magazines and television, everyone knows most of the great tourist attractions outside their own country. Niagara Falls, Hong Kong and the pyramids. The Eiffel Tower, the Colloseum and the Vatican in Rome. You may have read about these places, they may have been brought to your attention by a friend, or else you studied them at school. If pressed, most of us could compile a very long list.

A chateau in France, a European countries parliamentary building, the astronomical clock in Prague, the Isle of Capri, the Alps in Switzerland. Your secret wish could be to visit any of these places.

• LISTING THE SIGHTS YOU WOULD LIKE TO SEE.

Having compiled your list of potential tourist destinations reach a decision about which of them you really want to see. Be realistic. Exercise a little self-discipline and come up with a short-list which might reasonably match a tour on offer by the travel agent, which also fits within your allowed vacation time.

• WORKING OUT HOW MUCH MONEY YOU NEED TO TAKE.

Apart from the cost of the tour you eventually choose there are such things as flights to and from the departure point, personal spending each day, and optional tours while away which could average about 60 euro per day.

A good way to measure just exactly how much you are going to need to take overseas is to experiment at home first. Go to your largest city, or the most popular tourist destination in your country, and experience first hand how much is required for accommodation, transport, and eating in nice restaurants, drinks included. Add to that the cost of visiting the main attractions and the whole exercise will give you a very good understanding of how much you might spend when you get overseas.

I have found that no matter where I am in the world the admission prices to places of interest to me were all rather similar. I went to hear the Philharmonic Orchestra at the new Disney Hall in Los Angeles. Tickets cost between 40 and 120 U.S. dollars. If you were to go to a cabaret in Paris, depending on whether you had a meal or not, you would pay between 60 and 110 U.S. dollars. A cruise on the Sydney Harbour with dinner – but no drinks – and not including transport down to the docks, or tipping, would cost approximately 120 Australian dollars.

So armed with all this sort of information you'll have a very good idea how much money you'll need to take on your tour.

• SET YOUR GOAL FOR WHEN YOU WOULD LIKE TO TRAVEL.

Always try to travel when you really want to go. Some people choose the cheapest time to travel and as a result their trip can sometimes lack ambience and atmosphere. Work out what you want to see and how you want to see it. Fantasize a little. The idea of a great holiday for some is going to a place like Italy and experiencing the dolce vita by sitting on the piazzas, glass in hand, listening to beautiful music. And there's nothing wrong with that. But there's no point looking for this sort of thing in the dead of winter when most outdoor facilities have closed down and moved indoors. So don't let cost dictate something you may not want. It's usually best to travel in the warmer months.

Although, having said that, winter does have its attractive side in Europe. The countryside can be picture-perfect with snow blanketing everything, and there is skiing and ice skating available as well as a host of other winter attractions not necessarily available back home.

Winter travelling can be a lot of fun but there are a number of things to be aware of. There are a lot less daylight hours; you'll be leaving your hotel in the morning before the sun is up, and arriving back after the sun has gone down. In a place like Australia where winter daytime temperatures in the southern cities doesn't get much below 10°C, in a typical European city the temperatures could plummet to 1°C. European winters are traditionally far colder than those down under.

Some people reason that there is no point touring in winter trying to beat the cold each day. Others relish the prospect. They kit themselves out with the appropriate winter clothing bought on the European Continent because it is generally cheaper. More thermal underwear, woolen hats, scarves and gloves are needed in Europe so more are produced there than in a place where winters are not as cold. More need, more production, and more sales outlets means more competition. Hence more reasonable prices.

Things to trip you up.

If there is a particular sight that you absolutely positively definitely must see when you are in Europe then it would pay to do a little extra research to make sure it is going to be open when you are in the city where it is located. Although believe it or not even this will not guarantee you being able to make your visit. Some of the things that may get in your way are as follows ...

1   Various staff are on strike
2   Venue closed for impromptu renovations
3   Main exhibitions are on loan or on tour
4   Death of a famous person. May be closed out of
    respect to the deceased. You may remember when
    Gianni Versace was killed, all the shops were draped

with black and remained closed for a period of mourning.

Some of the more famous sites and closure days that may surprise you ...

1   Vatican Museum closed on a Sunday.
2   Palace of Versailles closed on a Monday.
3   Muse D'orsay closed on a Monday.
4   Claude Monet's house and gardens at Giverny closed on Mondays.
5   Louvre museum in Paris closed on a Tuesday
.

Incidental tour expenses.

There are many different items to take into account when reckoning the cost of a holiday, but the main thing is not to worry too much about any of them. The cost is the cost and worrying isn't going to change anything. To give you an idea how it works, and so that you are more aware of what is involved, I could compare going on tour with buying your first motor vehicle.

You were quite happy to pay over a few hundred dollars back then and probably drove off as proud as Punch. Then you suddenly realized that you had to buy petrol to make your vehicle run, and that from now on you'd have to set aside a few dollars each week for the purpose. Then the reality of other costs hit you. Such things as insurance and registration needed to be taken care of, and a set of tyres every couple of years or so.

Not to mention repairing the occasional damage or replacing some worn out part. But that's life. And life is all about continually having to pay out for little bits and pieces.

So with cars and homes which both need constant maintenance, and which both give back a lot of enjoyment, the money paid out is considered to be well worth it when you consider what you get back.

Travel is no different, depending on what you are looking for. You'll only get out of it what you're prepared to put in. Or put more bluntly, you'll only get what you pay for.

- ## TRANSFER FROM YOUR HOME TO THE AIRPORT.

Many cities have public buses or shuttle services to take you to your local airport. If you want to go a step higher you might like to make use of a taxi. But if it's a little more luxury you're after try a chauffeur-driven vehicle. There's something there for everyone. So what the traveller needs to do is take all these relevant costs and the time associated with getting to the airport into consideration when budgeting and planning.

- ## FLIGHTS TO STARTING DESTINATION, INCLUDING TAXES.

Many countries around the world nowadays are advertising discounted fares, and the traveller really needs to be aware just what a discounted fare entails.

The cheaper flights advertised are those with no possibility of you being able to change anything. You can't change the flight date. You can't change the schedule, or your seat number. Having purchased a flight ticket like this you are stuck with these limitations.

In some countries the travel companies or airlines are under an obligation to include taxes in their advertised fares, but in other countries they will not be under the same obligation. So when inquiring about prices for flights always ensure whether or not they include taxes.

Something I've learned from experience, having purchased many tickets for flights over the years in different countries, is that by the time you check with two or three places about flying you realize there is a successful and efficient formula for travelling, i.e. work out what you want to do, work out time and place of departures, work out where you want to go, and your arrival and departure dates from these places, go to the travel agent, tell them what you need, ask them about relevant fares and mention any preferences you may have about a particular airline. Then ask them if they can offer anything suitable, preferrably with a substantial discount, that can come close to matching what you are after.

You might have to accept a slight change or two but the travel agent will look at the fare you were hoping for, and look at your other requirements, and from there they might start making suggestions which could go something like this: 'Oh well, look. If you leave two days earlier the fare will be 400 dollars cheaper, or a couple of hundred, whatever the case may be. And there could be advantages to this. You can have a stop-over along the way to your destination, see another city with the few hundred dollars you have saved, and then go on.'

These are a few little things which need to be thought about but overall, with the very heavy competition which exists among the airlines, (current at the time of going to press), many airlines and many travel agencies don't have a lot of margin to work with and when you start comparing one with another you'll begin to find similar pricing structures wherever you go.

- ## VISAS THAT MAY BE REQUIRED.

Remember to allow and account for any visas you may need. Your travel agencies are the people who should be able to inform you correctly of visa requirements, and if you are under the assumption you need a visa, and then are informed that you do not, it's always worth getting it in writing, or getting some sort of print-out verifying the fact. If you have this document you can then go into the country concerned, visiting with the confidence of knowing that you have the correct information.

Also understand however, that from time to time there are snap changes depending on the international relations between different countries which may result in visas being suddenly required. The laws requiring this may only have been gazetted since your time of departure from home. In many cases where this has happened, countries which have brought in a new regime of visa requirements will offer the chance to purchase a visa at their point of entry. Once again this is just one of those things which happens from time to time. It's all part of the travel experience. Don't be put off by it, and certainly don't become angry with the country because of what is happening. It is more than likely they have been forced into this kind of action to recoup money they might have lost through trade embargoes, or some such.

Visas can be quite a complicated element of your holiday, sometimes being subject to the vagaries of international relations and trade problems. So make sure before setting out that you have the right visas and the right visa advice.

- **TRANSFERS FROM DESTINATION AIRPORT TO HOTEL.**

Once again, allow for these items in your budget. Some tour companies will include the cost of a transfer from the airport to the hotel, but also be aware that the transfers offered may be either early in the morning or late in the evening and may not necessarily suit you. If you do not have transfers included you can usually rely on shuttles and taxis to get you to your hotel. From Heathrow Airport to central London, for example, the fare in a traditional London cab could be from 35 to 45 English pounds. From Gatwick to central London you'd be looking at approximately 50 to 70 pounds.

There are various other alternatives of course. Fast trains will take you from the airports into central London and you may need to take only a short taxi ride to the hotel after that.

- **HOTEL ACCOMMODATION PRIOR TO ANY ONWARD TRAVEL, AND DOES THE PRICE INCLUDE LOCAL TAXES, TIPS TO STAFF, AND BREAKFAST?**

Always allow for hotel accommodation before and after your tour. Remember that if you are flying a substantial distance to the point where you are commencing your tour you might like to have a couple of nights' accommodation to rest up, to become acclimatized, and even to engage in a bit of retail therapy.

At the end of your travel plans many companies suggest that you don't make any forward travel plans on the day the formal part of your tour ends. There's a good reason for this. You may find that on the very last day a hiccup of some kind such as industrial action could prevent you from getting to your final drop off point at the time expected. Many tours come to an end at 5pm on the final day, especially those which conclude in London. Many operators will suggest that you don't book flights back to your own country at that time because of unforeseen events such as ferry strikes and the like which could throw all your arrangements into chaos. People have actually missed their flights under these circumstances so stay in town for another night or two and then fly out.

Many people, depending where they are from, will already have add-on taxes and tipping systems in place in their own countries. In America, many prices are advertised without local taxes which then need to be added to the bill. On top of that there is tipping as well. So when it comes to these items remember to allow for them in your budgeting.

Most tour companies have recommendations about tipping allowances of approximately 4 U.S. dollars per day for tour directors, 2 ½ U.S. dollars per day for drivers, and 2 U.S. dollars per day for local guides when used. Many of these rates translate easily into euro as well. So that you will pay 4 euro per day for tour directors, 2 ½ euro per day for drivers, 2 euro per day for local guides, and when it comes to tipping taxi drivers the rate has been set at around 10% of the fare. Restaurant tipping is probably the most expensive. This can be up to 20% of the total bill.

If you are travelling on a tour your tour director will give you the relevant information for the different countries you pass through.

Another thing to take into account is whether or not your hotel accommodation includes breakfast. If you are travelling in Europe a standard 'continental' breakfast will usually consist of a bread roll, a croissant, jam, ham and cheese, coffee and cereal and will quite often cost around 10 euro per person over and above the cost of your hotel accommodation. These are all quite small costs but they do have to be allowed for.

- TAXI TO DEPARTURE POINT IF A HOTEL PICK-UP IS NOT INCLUDED, AND SOME EXAMPLES OF PRICES.

If you are anticipating taking part in a European tour you might find that in London you'll need to allow about 10 English pounds to get to your departure point. If you are in other major European capitals some representative charges might be, around Paris, 15 to 20 euro, and in Rome, 30 euro. In fact allow up to 30 euro for any taxis you may need to take from one hotel to another in these large cities. But first check with reception at your hotel to get a reasonable idea what you might be in for.

- THE COST OF THE TOUR DAY BY DAY.

When it comes to the cost of a tour day by day you first need to look at the initial basic cost of the tour itself and divide by the number of days allocated for it. This could work out to be anywhere from 75 to 130 euro per day, depending on which tour you are taking. These costs will generally include all your accommodation as well as other items such as half of your dinners, all of your breakfasts, basic sightseeing, and the cost of local guides in major European cities. As well as that the cost will include the services of your tour director and your driver. You may, however, need to budget for tipping those providing the various services.

Other costs you'll need to budget for are things such as lunch, which is generally at your own expense, and will cost between 9 and 15 euro per day, and is a simple sit-down affair with maybe one drink included. Bearing in mind that city lunches are much more expensive that those in the smaller country towns. And then you will need to allow for a whole host of lesser expenses such as a coffee now and then, an ice cream in Italy, a cake in Budapest or Prague, both of which cities are famous for their cuisine, postcards, stamps, impulse purchases, telephone calls, films and so on.

I've always suggested to people when it comes to spending money in Europe that they allow 100 euro per person per day for all these things. This is a realistic figure taking into account things which you are most likely to do on a day to day basis to enjoy and get the most out of the various cities without feeling you are doing it too much on the cheap.

• BREAKFAST

Breakfast on many tours is included in the overall cost. If not, allow 10 euro per person per day for a simple continental, and possibly 15 to 20 euro per day for a buffet breakfast.

Once again, to familiarize yourself with some of these costs just go into any hotel back home, or phone them up and ask how much it would cost for a breakfast purchased independently of the cost of a room. They will be quite quick to tell you, and you may be surprised at what you are told.

It is not necessarily the cost of the croissant and coffee that is represented by the price. This is more a reflection of the owner buying and upkeeping the building around you while you sit there munching your croissant and sipping your coffee. It all had to be paid for and this infrastructure imposes itself on to the cost of whatever you are having for breakfast of necessity.

It is as well to remember though that the hotel owner and restaurant proprietor both have to live too.

- **MORNING COFFEE WITH PASTRY OR SANDWICH.**

The price of a cup of coffee in London will vary between 1 ½ pounds and 2 ½ depending on where you purchase it. In Paris a cup will cost between 2 and 5 euro once again depending on where you go. In Italy, the home of many different coffee drinks, the cost is also between 2 and 5 euro. Throughout the remainder of the European Union prices are similar. For a can or bottle of soft drink you can expect to pay anywhere between 2 and 5 euro.

The drinks can cost considerably more if consumed at some prestigious address. For example, a cup of coffee on the Piazza San Marco could set you back 10 euro. But if you just want a quick coffee standing up at a bar somewhere the price can be quite reasonable. Sit down at some place which has a view however and your drink price will rise quite significantly.

For sandwiches, baguettes, rolls or croissants or any other kind of light snack to go with your coffee you will pay from 3 to 6 euro, depending on what you order and where you intend eating it.

• LIGHT LUNCHES

Light lunches anywhere in Europe will cost approximately 10 to 15 euro.

• AFTERNOON SNACKS

Afternoon snacks consisting of something like a coffee and cake would run out at about 5 or 6 euro.

• DINNER INCLUDED BUT NOT DRINKS.

Dinner without drinks in most European countries will cost in the region of 35 to 45 euro as long as you don't order anything too extravagant. Entrees will cost between 7 to 10 euro, main courses 12 to 20 euro and desserts 8 to 10 euro.

On top of all these prices you need to allow for local taxes and service charges which could add up to 10% of the bill, or 15% in some countries, and even as high as 20% in a few others. So two people dining out together will find that they don't get much change out of 90 euro for something as simple as a basic three course meal and a couple of drinks.

Many hotels throughout Europe provide a three-course set dinner for around 30 euro but this price does not include service fees or drinks. For a few extra euro to the tour company at the beginning you can look forward to more up-market dinners valued at 55 to 60 euro per person which will not only include a four-course dinner, which is quite normal, but will also include a selection of different dishes you may wish to try, including beer, wine and soft drink.

It is important to realize however that when some companies offer a deal 'drinks included' they mean drinks of **their** choice and not of **your** choice. Some resorts will offer 'drinks included', but this refers only to their own in-house cocktail. When coach touring companies advertise 'drinks included' the drink in this case will normally be beer, wine, soft drinks and also water as well.

A point to make here is that most countries in Europe will provide bottled water on the table at an additional cost and it is quite interesting to note that in a lot of cases it's just as economical to drink beer or wine instead.

Some of the misunderstandings I've seen with travellers out on the town buying dinners involves those who do it alone in what is to them a foreign environment. They can spend a lot of unnecessary money doing this. And a lot of the problem has to do with language. They may have ordered a dish from the menu, it has been given an unexpectedly different description, and what they get isn't necessarily what they were expecting.

I sat in a restaurant once where I asked the waiter for what was in effect a bottle of house wine, expecting the price to be quite moderate. Unknown to me, a bottle of house wine in that particular establishment cost approximately 30 euro.

I've heard of people who ordered soup but when it came out it was little more than flavoured water. They later found out they had ordered a consomme, which is a light, clear soup flavoured only with meat, fish or vegetable stock popular on the Continent, but not so highly regarded in some other countries. They then ordered a steak which they thought sounded good on the menu, it had a tartare sauce or some such with it, only to discover that their steak tartare was in fact raw minced up fillet steak mixed with onions, capers, eggs and such, which is quite a traditional dish in France, for example. Unless you were familiar with the French language, and French cuisine, you could easily be forgiven for making such a mistake.

So, little experiences like these can drive up the cost of eating out and you only get to be restaurant savvy after years of experience at it.

When it comes to dining out on the Continent, and money is no object, you won't always mind if you don't get exactly what you were looking for. There can be an element of fun in this sort of thing.

But people on some kind of a budget need to seek guidance on some of these things rather than be too experimental. A lot of the time on tour there is quite a variety of different dishes on offer anyway and this does give the opportunity to the average traveller to try a new dish or two versus walking into a restaurant and having to order a la carte and not necessarily understanding the type of menu you are being offered.

Unfortunately, I find that when it comes to different cuisine a lot of people tend to go for the safety of a very familiar dish. And when you travel to the other side of the world this can be a bit of a shame.

• TAXI FROM YOUR HOTEL TO CITY, AND IS THERE A MINIMUM FARE?

Sometimes it can be quite a frustration for a lot of people when they go to order a taxi and find that some won't pick up from their hotel. The distance the taxi has to travel to get to you isn't economical. For this reason some taxi companies will impose a minimum fare despite the fact that you might only be wanting to travel about a kilometre. This minimum might be 6 or 8 euro. Another thing people get confused about is that in some countries you have to pay for the taxi to journey to where you are. Before the taxi arrives at your pick-up point there may already be 10 euro on the clock.

When it comes to taxis another thing to take into consideration throughout Europe is that taxi drivers prefer to take three people in their vehicle. If you are travelling as two couple you may find that you have to take two taxis. You may need to pay a premium for four people to travel in one taxi – should such an unlikely event occur.

You'll start to realize how the system works quite quickly when you go to enter the front seat of a taxi and the driver has newspapers, street directories, drinks and all sorts of thing on the front seat beside him. He's trying to tell you something. But don't be offended by this sort of things. It isn't anything personal. It's just the culture of that particular country.

Budgeting on holiday.

We all have budgets of one kind or another to work with and holidaying is no different. And as the saying goes 'one man's feast is another man's famine' so when it comes to budgeting be prepared to spend a little more than anticipated.

I am sure if you think back to some of your greatest memories or experiences which came as a result of stretching the credit card or bank balance, you'll agree that the memories from that time are now priceless. Yet if you tried to recall what the cost was you probably wouldn't be able to remember. Yet so often people worry about the cost rather than the benefit. My advice with regard to holiday budgeting is to do the saving before you leave home (which I will also try to offer some advice on as well) and when the time comes, spend like there is no tomorrow and enjoy yourself.

- **PHONE CALLS. IS THAT CHEAP PHONE CARD AS CHEAP AS IT LOOKS AND JUST HOW MUCH IS IT WORTH PAYING FOR CONVENIENCE?**

Many people have been talked into purchasing phone cards which offer very cheap phone calls around the world. An important point about these cards however is that people are finding when they get around to the other side of the world that some of the cards aren't as reliable as they initially thought. There are several reasons for this. Sometime the quality of the telephone line being used isn't up to scratch. Sometimes there might be a delay for one reason or another. And sometimes there is very heavy traffic on the line with the result that callers experience great difficulty trying to get through.

I have always suggested to people that the most effective way to make phone calls from other countries is to purchase a local phone card issued by the country you may for the time being find yourself in. These cards must be completely used up inside the country of purchase and cannot be taken over the border into a neighbouring country even though they are paid for in euro and both countries side by side use euro. So it's a matter of purchasing a card, making your call, and then throwing the card away. Doing this is the closest guarantee you'll get to a clear line and minimum delay.

With a clear line you'll probably say all you have to inside five minutes anyway, but fifteen minutes might be required to say something on a line that is way below par. Under these circumstances you keep needing to repeat and re-iterate what you just said. And this sort of thing can happen with a cell phone too. The signal will fade. There will be interference, and a simple call can drag on and on. And this is what it is like with some of the cheaper cards. So be aware of what you are purchasing before you go away.

- **BOTTOM LINE. SPEND YOUR MONEY ON YOURSELF AS YOU ARE THE ONE WHO**

WORKED AND SAVED HARD TO BE ON THE HOLIDAY.

From my experience I see many people come from the other side of the world and upon arrival, get all bent out of shape over all the presents they need to buy for friends and relations back home. Many people farewelled them at the start of their journey by pressing a shopping list into their hand and when I suggest to the tourist that he or she join the group and come out for a nice dinner they inform me that they haven't got the money.

I always suggest to people in this situation that they continue thinking about those back home but not make them the whole emphasis of their holiday.

For people back home who have not travelled I ask that you don't send your friend or family member away on what is supposed to be the holiday of their lifetime with great long shopping lists. Even though you have given them money. A lot of the time many of the requested items can be purchased just as cheaply back in your own country, and it's a little bit unfair to impose such demands on people who have worked hard and only have a limited time in each country. They deserve to enjoy their time away. Please try not to unintentionally monopolize it in any way.

But don't get to feel that your travelling friend isn't thinking of you. Just realize that this is the person who worked hard and saved to go away. And anything they do bring back for you should be treated as a bonus. So try not to be too demanding.

And for you people who do go away, use your money to spend on yourself because it's a shame to have travelled all the way to the other side of the world only to find that you are spending your whole time working out how you are going to please everybody back home.

Because if you do, when you get back from a trip like this you won't even feel as though you've had a holiday.

Choosing a travel agent.

When it come time to choose a travel agent look for someone who has experience, and someone who knows what they are talking about. In theory, if you read this book before you go to the travel agent ask them a few simple questions about whether they have been to the place you intend visiting. Stretch their mind a little and try to gauge whether you are in the right place. Not every travel agent can know everything about every product but a good agent will try to find out for you the answer to any travel questions which for the time being may not be known him/her.

There are many travel agents who take on too much work and unfortunately don't get to give a good quality of service. The problem might be pressure from their employers, or they just might not be very organized.

You'll find there are excellent travel agents, average travels agents, and unfortunately some not so good travel agents. But you'll get this thing in every walk of life and in every profession. So don't be afraid to assertively 'interview' two or three travel agents with a standard list of questions. Ask them about optional tours. Ask them about approximately how much money you should be spending and you should find that if they are thinking along the same lines as yourself you both should come up with similar sorts of ideas.

It's a good idea to come up with a travel agent who suits your needs and **is** going to think like you do. There's no point going to a travel agent who specializes in luxury first class tours if all you want to do is go on a back-packing holiday. So try to match your needs with a travel agent who can supply those needs. And also understand that many of the travel agents will only answer the questions you ask. Quite often I've said to people 'did your travel agent tell you about this?' and the answer was 'no' but the reason the travel agent hadn't told them was because the people hadn't requested the information.

I've worked in travel agencies and have many friends who are still involved in travel agencies around the world and one thing we were taught to assume when someone walked in the front door and told us 'I want to take a fifteen day tour, and I want this, and I want that' was that they already knew what they wanted so you didn't have to volunteer a whole lot of information or extend the conversation in any way. You simply took their deposit and gave them a receipt. So be aware of this.

3

PREPARING TO GO AWAY

A suitable amount of preparation before departure can really make a difference to the enjoyment of your holiday. By being properly prepared you can avoid the expense of unnecessary and impromptu purchases which often carry a high premium.

The following two websites are worth looking at before departure too. Both offer advice on the many different facets of travel and you don't need to be a citizen of the two countries to benefit.

- The Australian government website.
  www.smarttraveller.gov.au

- U.S. State Department, which issues travel warnings for all parts of the world.
  www.travel.state.gov/travel_warnings.html

When considering identification you should always carry colour photos of all family members accompanying you, as well as photocopies of your passport identification pages and copies of your credit card details (colour if possible). Digital cameras are great for this as you can take a photo of all your documents and burn them to disc to take away with you. And should you require them to be printed there is an increasing number of photographic stores which will offer this service. Or if you only need to reference the information many of the large hotels will have a business centre where you can use a computer.

It can be worthwhile too to have a couple of driver licence copies made up by laminating them in case of loss or theft (they are also handy to give as identification and of you forget to get them back or they are taken as souveniers it does not matter as much). Any items of extreme monetary or sentimental value should be left at home in a safe place or if necessary, locked away in a bank security box. And it would certainly be worth your while setting up a telephone or internet banking facility. Or at the very least, make sure that the decision maker at your local bank knows you are going away and will be able to assist you with your banking while you are overseas.

Make up an emergency card with all your emergency telephone and fax numbers, and e-mail addresses. And it may be worthwhile having a medical check-up before departure to make sure no short term health problems are likely to arise.

Children travelling with parents should have their own identity cards in case they get lost or separated. They should have some form of emergency bracelet or id card which should say such things as 'I am lost. Please tell a member of the police,' or 'please call this number to contact my parents'. This is best written in the language of the country of which you are travelling. At the very least you should write this in English, but at the very minimum make sure the children have something with emergency contact telephone numbers.

They should also at all times have on their person a copy of their home address and a full list of hotels (and their telephone numbers) you will be staying at while away. Also include the dates of your stay at each place and the telephone number of your travel company and your tour director if you are touring as part of a group.

Before you leave home.

For people who are not frequent users of hotels it sometimes comes as a surprise that many hotels will not allow you to check in until after two or three o'clock in the afternoon. And if you have arrived at the airport around seven in the morning and gotten to the hotel at nine or ten it can be very frustrating to discover this. Especially if you have come off a long flight and have been in the same clothes now for many hours.

A couple of suggestions to combat this are to contact the hotel before departure from your home town informing them of your early arrival, and while understanding their check-in policy you would appreciate that should any rooms become vacated early and cleaned, you would like one to be allocated to you. They will normally be very non-committal and inform you that while not being able to give any guarantees your request has been noted.

You should then ask them for their name and then thank them by their name for being helpful, and then hope for the best.

Secondly, you should be prepared for your request not to be met, remembering that it is only a request and not a guarantee.

By having easily accessible something to use to freshen up you should then be able to store your luggage and then get out for a walk in a local park to get some fresh air, or sit in the park and enjoy some coffee or breakfast.

The only way to guarantee a room on arrival is to also pay for the night preceding the day of your arrival.

- **SOME OF THE OTHER SECURITY MEASURES YOU MAY WISH TO TAKE CARE OF BEFORE LEAVING HOME ARE AS FOLLOWS ...**

When it come to securing your home before you depart you may wish to consider having dead locks fitted to your exterior doors and key operated locks to your windows that are a little more vulnerable. If you have ever locked yourself out and had to get into your own home by breaking in you'll begin to appreciate just how easy it is. So you should certainly consider the above for your peace of mind. You might also find these measures could reduce the cost of your home insurance.

It is a good idea to have timers fitted to the lights. And outside to have sensor lights fitted to the front and rear of the house.

Cut back any overgrown trees or shrubs that may provide cover for someone trying to break in.

Make sure that all outside sheds and garages have secure locks in place. You may also wish to chain and padlock any gates.

Make sure that your home and contents insurance is up to date. Recently purchased items may have increased the cover you should have. Check with your insurance company about this, and the fact that you are about to leave your home unattended for a period of time.

Inform the police of your departure and return dates.

Try to keep the curtains mainly drawn or ask a family friend to pop over once in a while to adjust the curtains so that the house looks lived in.

Always put expensive items out of view should someone be looking through your windows and if possible take a photograph of your most valuable items for insurance records.

Employ a lawn mowing service if you plan being away for more than a few weeks so the house will look as though it is being maintained.

You may also consider a monitored alarm system for your house.

Empty your fridge in case there is a power cut during your absence. A good way of doing this is to put on a small farewell party for yourself to use up all the food.

Turn off the gas supply to your house.

Get a neighbour to clear your mail box each day.

The countdown

One year before ....

1 Start to enquire about possible holiday options.
2 Make a list of what you want to see and do.
3 Start telling people what you plan to do. This will allow friends and family to plan any special events around your time away.
4 Set a goal of how much spending money you want to take after allowing for transport and accommodation. I suggest 150 euro per day for an absolutely fantastic time.
5 Consider a part time job to boost your savings. This will benefit you in two ways. Firstly, you will earn some extra money and secondly, while you are working at your extra job you will have less time to be out spending the money you are now saving.

6   Another way to save money is to leave the house with just enough cash to cover the needs of the day. This will stop you spending more than you intended. Leave the credit cards at home too. This is the time to be saving your money.

7   Purchase a book on how to minimize your living costs without sacrificing too much of your lifestyle.

8   Make a record of your weekly expenditure and after one week sit down and work out what can be reduced. This money can then be put towards the holiday.

9   Start taking your lunch to work.

10 Start taking vacuum flask of coffee to work.

11 If you do not normally cook at home take cooking lessons so that you can start making attractive dishes at home. This will reduce the need to go to restaurants. You will also meet some nice people at the classes and learn about the food of the countries you may wish to visit.

12 Purchase a good book on your destination country. This will whet your appetite for the holiday and enhance the experience when it finally takes place.

Six months before ...

1   Check your progress on all of the above.

2   Check passport validity and make sure it will remain valid for at least six months after you return home. If not, now is the time to look at renewing. If you need

help with this a good travel agent should have everything you need to know.

3 Start to narrow down your dates.

4 Enquire about any visas you may need but do understand that visa regulations can change literally at a moment's notice.

5 If you have settled on a final travel date make your booking.

6 Ask if the departure is guaranteed.

7 Keep an eye out for luggage on sale, bearing in mind luggage restrictions of the travel company or airline. Most travel companies restrict luggage to one suitcase of a reasonable size per person. Sometimes these sizes will be stated in the brochure.

8 Start to familiarize yourself with e-mail and the internet if these are foreign to you. This will give you time to send some practise e-mails.

WE ARE STARTING TO GET CLOSE NOW SO WE HAD BETTER MENTION SOME THINGS NOT TO TAKE.

---

1 Currency converter. A normal calculator will do, and you may even think twice about taking this, because just about anywhere it is possible to spend money the minute you even think about making a purchase – and sometimes even before – you will feel a gentle breeze blow past you which is usually created by a lightning quick whipping movement of a sales person's fingers over their calculator as they proceed

to tell you the relevant cost of the item in at least half a dozen currencies.

2 Many people who have travelled will recognize however that with the introduction of the euro the skill of producing the total in fifteen currencies in under a minute, is slowly becoming obsolete.

3 A huge overcoat if travelling in winter. You will do better with several layers of suitable clothing such as winter fleece and thermal underwear, (these are all available from large camping shops) or a silk 'T' shirt, also a new thermal under and overwear products on the market is called "Icebreaker" and could be worth a look at www.icebreakernz.com. The big overcoats are very bulky and if they get soaked can be a nightmare to dry out. I would hate to even guess at the cost of dry cleaning one at a hotel. If you need to take a coat get a three-quarter one or a car coat which won't drag through the mud or take up as much room.

Three months before ...

1 Book your holiday if you have not already done so.

2 Think about doing a bit of walking. You might wish to start with around thirty minutes a day. Many of the old cities of the world have restricted access and therefore you will be required to walk a bit and use stairs. This is something which surprises many people so if you can get your fitness level up a little

you will not only get more out of your holiday, you will also feel better.

3   Start to look passively at travel gadgets, adapters, money belts, travel clotheslines and such.

Two months before ...

1   Start getting excited if you haven't already.

2   Read at least one book on the areas through which you will be travelling.   If you have a little background on these places it can make the experience a little more rewarding.

3   If you are planning to buy some good sturdy shoes now is the time to do it so you can break them in before going away.   Get some professional advice and buy the best you can afford.   As my good friend Nick told me once: 'Craig, buy the best shoes, and the best bed you can afford.   Because mate, if you're not in one you'll be in the other'.   I followed Nick's advice and bought the best shoes I could afford because when I am working I spend up to eighteen hours a day in them.   And fortunately, they feel like slippers.

One month before ...

1   Place a medium size box somewhere in the house so that every time you come across something that needs to be taken with you it can go in the box.   This will reduce the pressure of rushing to pack at the last minute.

2   Tell your doctor your plans and request any medication you may need to take away. Always try to take with you double the amount in case you lose one of your bags.

3   See the bank about increasing your credit card limit to the maximum amount possible.

4   Start preparing an emergency medical kit containing the following items ...

(a) Bandaids, and blister relief patches. I suggest a Company by the name of Compeed. Their 'Second Skin' patches are amazing. They have always done the job for both myself and my clients over the years.

(b) Strong painkillers. See your doctor for these. There is nothing worse than getting toothache and not having something to get you through until you reach a dentist.

(c) An antiseptic in case you cut yourself.

(d) Another handy item, especially if you are travelling to areas where the water quality is a bit dubious, is an intestinal antiseptic. (I believe the active ingredient is nifuroxazide). If you have a delicate stomach this will keep you regular while combating any nasties. I escorted a group of nearly forty people to Egypt and suggested they purchase this and begin taking it one week before arriving in that country to build up their immunity. After a few days in Egypt a high proportion of people who seemed to have problems had not purchased this antiseptic and were now paying for it.

(e) Multivitamins.

(f) Also have some Imodium tablets but only use in an emergency as I have found that they block you up and make you feel bloated. A good idea is to speak to a doctor or pharmacist about these.

(g) Sun tan lotion. In Europe it can be difficult to find S.P. Factor 30 blockout.

(h) Antihistamine cream for allergies and mosquito bites.

(i) Personal items such as contraceptives and tampons are best brought from your own country as sometimes production standards can vary around the world. For example in the Latin countries a large motor engine is three litres whereas in the Germanic countries a big engine is maybe five or six litres. So what may be considered large in one part of the world may only be medium in the other. You will also find the same with clothing as you move from country to country.

Three weeks before departure ...

1   Inform the paper delivery of your time away.
2   Inform your neighbours of your plans and exchange phone numbers with them so they can notify you or your family should they notice something amiss with your house or property.

3   Order traveller's cheques and foreign currency before leaving home as money changing facilities at airports can charge a premium. Consider shopping around for these as the exchanges can vary significantly.

4   Get some passport photos.

5   Set up mail redirection to a friend to avoid mailbox overflow, also consider asking the post office to hold your mail.

6   Notify anyone involved with items to be delivered to your house.

7   Organize with a gardener to maintain lawns if going away for more than a month or so.

Two weeks before departure ... Check some essentials to take away ...

1   ☐   Tickets.
2   ☐   Passports.
3   ☐   Traveller's cheques.
4   ☐   Credit cards.
5   ☐   Some cash for arrival in first country.
6   ☐   Emergency number list.
7   ☐   Reading material for the aircraft.
8   ☐   Finalize packing list.
     ☐   Money belt which can be concealed beneath clothing, whether around waist or around neck. At all cost try to avoid the slowly-going-out-of-fashion bumbag or fanny pack, as it is called, or you might as well draw a

bullseye on it and write: 'money here. Please come and get it'.

9 ☐ One small travel umbrella per person to avoid complications of sharing if travelling with a partner. You may wish to see different sights.

10 ☐ A poncho or raincoat can be very handy and doesn't take up much room.

11 ☐ Portable washing line.

12 ☐ A bar of laundry soap for hand washing small items.

13 ☐ Small vacuum flask for hot liquids – water, coffee, soup.

14 ☐ Immersion heater for boiling water in your own room.

15 ☐ Some coffee sachets and/or teabags.

16 ☐ Small spoon for stirring. Perhaps the disposable one used on the flight for stirring your coffee?

17 ☐ A small hip flask if you like a snifter on the road.

18 ☐ Any adapters you may need for all electrical items you are carrying.

19 ☐ Any transformers for above. Europe uses 240 volt electricity.

20 ☐ Travel alarm clock.

21 ☐ A small flashlight or a candle in case of a blackout in the hotel.

22 ☐ A simple, but reliable watch. And think about getting a new battery in it before you leave.

23 ☐ Batteries for video or digital cameras and photo storage cards, memory sticks, and the like.

24 ☐ Batteries for any other battery operated items.

25 ☐ Sunglasses and prescription glasses.

26 ☐ Suitable travel sock for long haul flights to help circulation.

27 ☐ One set of good clothes for a nice night out.

28 ☐ Two pairs of good sturdy walking shoes in a slightly larger size than normal. Your feet will swell on aircraft journeys of long duration, or in summer on long bus trips. One of the pairs can double as dress shoes, doing away with the need to pack fancy footwear which might hardly be used. Apart from anything else, it is easier to wear walking shoes to a cabaret in Paris than to climb the stairs of the Colliseum in high heeled shoes.

29 ☐ A pair of slippers for use in showers or around hotel swimming pools.

30 ☐ Five pairs of cotton sox.

31 ☐ Eight sets of underwear.

32 ☐ Four lots of bottom clothes, i.e. pants, jeans or shorts for mean, or pants, jeans, shorts, skirts for ladies. Men may wish to pack two pairs of dark cotton pants as they are lighter and more comfortable than denim and dry quicker if you need to wash them.

33 ☐ Six lightweight cotton shirts and a mix of long and short sleeves depending on season of travel.

34 □   One undershirt or 'T' shirt for wearing on dress down days or travel days. One lightweight jacket.

35 □   Toiletries bag.

36 □   Soap holder if necessary. You can also wrap soap in an old stocking or mesh to make it last longer.

37 □   Facecloth if desired, as many hotels do not provide these.

One week before departure ...

1   Do a preliminary pack of your suitcase today.

2   Make sure luggage is labelled with all relevant information and if you have the standard black luggage put a distinguishing piece of ribbon on it so it can be easily recognizable in the luggage carousel.

3   Remove half of your clothing from the suitcase and leave it behind. Especially if you already think you have packed too much.

4   Leave room for souvenirs.

5   Double the amount of money you thought you would spend. Especially if you think you will do it cheaper than I am suggesting, while still experiencing all that is on offer.

6   Finalize emergency contact list if not already completed.

Five days before departure ...

Do your final pack today and weigh your suitcase. You should be able to pick it up, or at least roll it around the house comfortably – unless of course you plan on travelling with a servant.

Three days before departure ...

1 Pick up any dry cleaning.
2 Don't eat any hot, spicy or unusual foods from now until you depart. You don't want to fly with a funny tummy.
3 Start eating slightly lighter meals so you don't feel bloated on the plane.

Two days before departure ...

1 Do your final pack today if not already done.
2 Make sure luggage is labelled.

Put aside things to carry on your person ...

1 Passport.
2 Cash.
3 Traveller's cheques
4 Tickets and itinerary summary.
5 Special needs or tampons for ladies. You never know how your system may react to a new routine. Over the years I have had many requests for emergency supply.
6 Two Immodium tablets in case you need them in transit. Funny tummies have blatant disregard for a traveller's timetable.
7 Money belt to put all the above into.

8   Phone card and dialing information, if you have one.
9   Sunglasses.
10 Business cards if you have them, very handy for passing on your details to people.
11 Address and phone number of accommodation at first port of call.
12 Have some coins for the airport in case you need to hire a trolley for your luggage.

And also put aside your clothes for the flight ...

1   Loose-fitting and breathable items.
2   Loose-fitting shoes.
3   Travel socks.
4   Light jacket.

And your carry-on luggage ...

1   A copy of this book. Your journey has now begun so keep a record of your experiences for the future and remember that this is not a rehearsal but that every day is one show only with no repeats.
2   Change of clothes. In case your main luggage is lost on route.
3   Basic toiletries, toothbrush and toothpaste. However no sharp objects such as nail files, tweezers or small scissors.
4   Basic first aid kit.
5   Set of plastic gloves.
6   Camera.

7   A couple of plastic bags. These are great for carrying any overflow from your hand luggage.
8   Prescriptions and medication.
9   Earplugs to dull airplane engine noise and eye shades for sleeping.
10 Refresher towels or moisturiser towels.
11 Reading material for the plane.
12 Some snacks. However, don't try to carry food into another country. Quarantine can be very strict and your trip could end before it even gets started. If you are not sure, declare it and ask Customs.

The day before ...

1   Wear clothes you are not taking with you.
2   Lay out in one area all the things to be carried on your person.
3   Prepare what you will wear on the plane.

The night before ...

GET A GOOD NIGHTS SLEEP.

Packing Tips

Mark each piece of luggage independently on the outside with address of destination, mobile phone numbers, and your e-mail address.

Write your mobile phone number with any international codes included so you may be contacted directly should the luggage go astray. For example, the plus symbol should precede all phone numbers, followed by your country access code, then the city code and finally, your private number.

- SOME EXAMPLES FOLLOW ...

1. +61 2 99999999 - Sydney, Australia landline.
2. +61 8 88888888 - Adelaide, Australia landline.
3. +61 418 00000 - Australian Mobile.
4. +1 211   - Los Angeles, USA landline.
5. +1   - New York landline.
6. +1 402 9999999 - Omaha, Canada landline.
7. +64 9   - Auckland, New Zealand landline.
8. +64 21   - New Zealand mobile.

Put the address of a friend or workplace on the luggage tags, but not the address of the house which will be left vacant during the holiday.

Put emergency items such as medicines, toiletries and a set of underwear into carry-on luggage.

Pack half and half if travelling with a friend or spouse, so that if in the unfortunate event of a suitcase getting lost it won't be a complete disaster. Although having to suffer a temporary inconvenience at least you will be able to continue your journey until reunited with your luggage.

Getting to the airport.

If on an early flight book a taxi at least one day in advance and ask the taxi company to call thirty minutes before the taxi's arrival. This serves two purposes. It is a back-up wake-up call, and secondly it assures you that your taxi is coming. Also ask the taxi company for a fixed price fare to the airport and in addition, make sure you get the taxi controller's name. Also, have the correct money for your journey available to give to the taxi driver.

It always amazes me how many taxi or private hire drivers and chauffeurs never have any change when dropping clients at the airport for departures. It's an old trick, as they know you are generally in a hurry and despite being annoyed at the lack of change you are not wanting to miss your flight so you leave them the change from a fifty even though the fare was maybe only thirty five or forty. You reason that some things are just not worth the hassle and you will remember for next time. You remember back to the old saying that the school of life experience is the best education you can get – but often the fees are very high.

In conclusion, allow plenty of time for your journey to the airport in case Murphy's Law touches you. Examples of this can be flat tyre on car, ran out of fuel, sheep on the road in the country, got stuck waiting for a freight train, another vehicle ran into us at the lights.

EUROPEAN HEAVEN AND HELL

Heaven is where the cooks are French, the mechanics German, the police are British, the lovers are Italian and its all organized by the Swiss.

Hell is where the mechanics are French, the police German, the British are the cooks, the Swiss are the lovers and its all organized by the Italians.

4

YOU'RE ON YOUR WAY

Arrival at the first hotel.

For most travellers arriving at the first hotel in a new country they have never visited before and do not speak the language, the experience can be quite daunting. It's a bit like being re-born. Many will start their conversation with: 'excuse me, do you speak English?' However, a point almost always overlooked by people in this situation is that no matter how slowly you speak and how much you try to add their local accent to your dialogue they will not understand you at all – unless of course, they actually speak English in the first place. So let me repeat this so that you are absolutely sure not to make the second and third mistake of some travellers by trying to speak slower than at first and then increasing the volume in the hope that as your words are now louder they will permeate the tissue of the reception staff's skull. And hopefully, as these louder more slowly spoken and accented words enter their brain receptors they will be translated perfectly into the local tongue. Because this will not happen, and you will achieve the same result as beating your head against a brick wall, try something else.

I have found the best way to determine whether somebody speaks your language is to first of all greet them in their native tongue in a cheerful and friendly manner no matter how bad your attempt at speaking their language may be. More often than not they will appreciate the gesture and reciprocate with their attempt at your language.

Many people fail to understand that if the person you are trying to speak to is not completely confident in your language then they will be reluctant to try until you have first shown your willingness.

Because after all, YOU ARE NOT ONLY A GUEST, YOU ARE A VISITOR, hence the name 'Visitors' Visa', and not 'Guest Visa'.

• HOW THEY SEE YOU.

For most reception staff working in any hotel associated with international tourism and located in a city which is a point of arrival or departure for international tourists they find that their guests fall into several different categories. The most stressed guests are those who have just arrived from a foreign land. And we need to remember that the stress associated with travel to and in a foreign land, and the complication of even small things like working a phone, is enough to send some peoples' pulses racing.

The hotel staff might deal with many such stressed clients over the course of a day, and the stress can be caused by many other factors outside their control. For example, the client's luggage lost by the airline, clients whose booking has been made for the wrong day, clients who are not happy with the fact that the motorway is so close to their hotel room that they can see what type of cigarettes the drivers are smoking and clients who are simply tired and feeling a little bit overwhelmed by all the new things their brain is trying to digest.

If you do begin to feel stressed just remember that it is quite possible that the hotel staff are too.

So how do you make a difference? Try to speak the local language and the locals will be friendly to you. But don't be overly familiar. What you may see as normal, such as a word or gesture offered in the hope that it may help out may in fact have the opposite effect. The locals may see your word or gesture as being a little bit rude. Some examples follow ...

The fig gesture in Latin American countries is considered phallic and very rude. In Brazil it means good luck whereas in the North Americas it is a children's game and played for fun it means 'I have got your nose'.

In some countries, to turn your glass upside down on the bar is to mean that you have finished drinking, but in some pubs in Australia finishing your drink and turning the glass upside down and placing it on the bar may be construed to mean that you believe you can win a fight with anyone present.

The O.K. symbol is possibly one of the most versatile of all. In many western countries it simply means that everything is O.K. However in Brazil, Germany and Russia it indicates a private orifice and is considered very rude and insulting. In Japan it means that you would like your change in coins, while in France, to show this to someone is seen to be insulting as it denotes the number zero, or speaks of something considered to be worthless. And if placed over the nose it means to be drunk or intoxicated.

- ## WHY DON'T SOME HOTELS HAVE TOWELS AND SOAP IN THE ROOMS?

Sometimes chambermaids in some hotels forget to put towels and soap in the rooms but this is a rare occurrence. Usually on the tourist circuit those establishments who deal with tour groups on a regular basis have discovered that certain types of groups have a habit of pilfering as mentioned below, the hotels have therefore implemented a policy of not putting towels and soap in the rooms until the groups arrive, and what they'll do then is issue these items only on request. And there is a very good reason for this. In the past, hotel guests have been prone to spiriting towels and soap away in their suitcases and then going down to reception complaining that there are no towels in the room. This is almost impossible for hotel staff to verify one way or the other and so a new set of towels is issued.

But now the usual practice is to issue towels and soap to each room only when asked for by the guest. The items are signed for, and of course when the guest leaves again the items are signed off. This procedure means that less towels leave the hotel illegally. The hotel's losses because of light-fingered guests can be considerable over a twelve month period but the signing on and off for towels has made a big difference. The policy also largely eliminates the confusion of whether there were towels in the room or not to begin with.

- **HYGIENE. THE DIFFERENCE BETWEEN CLEAN AND DIRTY, AND DIRTY AND OLD.**

There are many hotels throughout the world which may not be more than a couple of years old but despite this it is obvious at a glance that their cleaning processes are not very effective. The buildings have managed to take on an aged appearance despite the fact that they are not old.

On the other hand there are hotels which really are quite old but which are still functioning reasonably well and their accommodation and facilities are clean and hygienic.

With regard to hygiene in other countries, what you may see as clean others may regard as not so clean, and vice versa. So do understand that people have many different ways of living and looking at things. So do be prepared for these differences and unless the differences are extreme, try to not focus too much attention on these things.

- ## IS IT A SERVIETTE A TOWEL OR A NAPKIN?

The answer to this question has largely to do with language misunderstandings. Objects such as serviettes, towels and napkins can mean different things to different people and in other languages can have many different connotations. For example, if you were to ask for a serviette in France you would actually receive a towel. And if you asked at reception for a towel they would gaze at you and wonder what you were talking about. And in some countries a serviette is called a napkin, and vice versa. It's all a play on words, depending on which country you come from.

- ## ASKING FOR EXTRA TOWELS FOR YOUR ROOM.

If you do need to ask for extra towels for your room it's always best to go to reception, as opposed to telephoning for them, and wait at reception until the towels materialize. Otherwise it's a case of out of sight, out of mind. If you stand there as a constant reminder of your request you'll be attended to much quicker, otherwise you might have to wait quite a long time. Most importantly however is try not to get frustrated if things take a little longer than you thought.

Hotel Dining.

- ## STEALING BREAKFAST. WHY WE DO IT AND WHY WE SHOULD NOT DO IT.

When it comes to food and associated costs in Europe or other tourist destinations some people find that the costs are going to be a little more expensive than they thought they were going to be. So at breakfast they resort to wrapping up food inside napkins and taking it away for lunch later. This is actually theft and most hotels have a very intolerant attitude towards this kind of activity, and it can be quite embarrassing if you are caught doing it.

It's always best to give yourself plenty of time when you come down to breakfast and whatever you feel you would like to eat help yourself and take it. But not outside the breakfast room wrapped in a napkin. This kind of theft in hotels is just another factor that forces up the cost of touring because hotels are being forced into the position of having to elevate their rates to compensate.

- **THE 'INCLUDED DINNERS'. WE GIVE YOU THE GOOD NEWS AND THE BAD NEWS.**

With group touring, the reality is that the included dinners are usually quite simple and the subject is the source of a number of jokes. A friend of mine has a story he never tires of telling people to the effect that the food is terrible – and that's the bad news – but the good news however is that you never get much to eat anyway. It isn't quite this bad of course. Generally there is a good, wholesome, three-course meal involved – with drinks available at an extra cost, and within the course of the included tour the meal is quite adequate and reasonable – the important thing to remember is that if you were ordering and paying for the meal independently you can very soon find yourself paying 25 to 30 euro for a meal of similar quality.

- **NORMALLY NO DRINKS ARE INCLUDED.**

The reason drinks are not included in the tour cost is that drinking is an optional activity and by not including them is just another way of keeping tour costs down. A general rule of thumb is that if any drinks are brought to the table, and the waiter has to remove a cap or cork, you will be charged for that particular drink.

The 'no-drinks-included' policy does, however, normally allow tap water with meals. Tap water in Europe is generally quite drinkable and not the health issue it can be in other parts of the world.

Dining out.

- **HOW TO PICK A GOOD RESTAURANT. WHAT DO THE SERVICE STAFF EXPECT FROM YOU AND WHAT SHOULD YOU EXPECT FROM THEM?**

In this book no specific recommendations have been made regarding restaurants and places of accommodation. The idea in these pages being more to educate people about what to look for, and what to be on guard against while on their travels, as opposed to giving them recommendations about where to sleep and eat.

When trying to determine the quality of an eating establishment look for a well maintained front-of-house, i.e. flowers in summer, clean windows in winter, and a well-swept pavement out front. If at all possible, try to eat in restaurants which have open kitchens so you can see the level of hygiene they operate under. If you are not sure, check the bathroom facilities. Spotless clean here will generally mean spotlessly clean everywhere. If the face the restaurant shows to the public each day is clean, then the whole building will likely be clean. And of course the reverse is true as well. If the part of the premises you can see is dirty and untidy, what on earth is it going to be like in those areas you can't see? You have to ask yourself these questions.

So look for an eating facility you feel comfortable going in to. Somewhere you feel comfortable ordering in. Somewhere that is clean, warm and inviting. Somewhere that is well lit. And somewhere which boasts a good quality of furnishing. Much of the time you will find that proprietors who invest in these things will also be making an investment in the production of high quality food. Also try to eat in a busy venue because the food will be turning over quicker and there will be less risk of being given anything sub-standard.

Unfortunately, if you haven't booked a table in some of the better restaurants – and it can be hard to find a good restaurant in Europe – you might find yourself being seated in a place that the locals usually shun.

When it comes to the use of restaurants the more reasonable priced ones are quite often located just off the main squares and you will find that in these areas you can find reasonable meals at reasonable prices however you will not necessarily be in the most popular of places. But if all you are looking for is a decent meal this should be fine. When it comes to dining on main squares in large tourist cities unfortunately some venues can rely purely on the demand of people to fill their venue each night and therefore do not need to concentrate as much on attention to detail on the quality of their food, so do be aware of this, you pay for the ambiance and not the quality of the food in these areas.

Calling home.

- ## CALL RATES AND THE CHEAPEST WAY.

The best way to use the local telecommunications companies is to use their phone cards which will usually be available at reception in the various hotels, at tobacconists, and at newspaper stands. They are also obtainable at various service stops spaced at intervals along the highways.

- ## BE PREPARED FROM HOME.

Be prepared from home to set up a calling card which you can actually use to call back to your own country when it becomes necessary. Organize this some months before leaving home. Calling cards can be set up at no cost to yourself so depending on where you are travelling to from your own country. Make sure you check with your own telephone service provider.

- ## IS THAT A DIAL TONE, OR AN ENGAGED SIGNAL?

It's easy to be confused by the different phone tones you are likely to hear in Europe and elsewhere. After dialing the numbers, a wait of twenty to thirty seconds is sometimes required before anything positive happens. Sometimes you will find in some countries that a signal which you would take for an engaged tone in your own country is in fact a ringing tone in another country. So be aware that there are differences and if you are not sure what is going on just ask your tour director.

- ## IF YOU HAVE TO CALL FROM YOUR ROOM MAKE SURE IT IS QUICK. COSTS CAN SURPRISE.

If you do have to make a telephone call from your own hotel room it's always a good idea to be on and off the phone as quickly as possible. Hotel phone calls can be very expensive; anything up to 10 euro per minute. It seems an extortionate cost when you have only been on the phone a couple of minutes and then there's a phone charge on the bill for 20 or 30 euro.

Once again from my own experience, I was staying at a hotel in Las Vegas and made a call from my room which lasted no more than three minutes. The cost was 36 U.S. dollars. Which taught me a valuable lesson. So if you are carrying a mobile, try texting your friends back home and don't forget to include the telephone number of the hotel you are staying at and include your room number as well.

- **BREAK THE CORNER OFF ITALIAN PHONE CARDS.**

One of the quirky little things about overseas telecommunication technology is the Italian phone card. When you purchase one of these you will see that it has a perforated corner on it, and this should be snapped off before the card is inserted into the phone. Otherwise nothing will be activated.

Shopping duty free and customs.

For some people on tour there is never enough shopping time. Yet some of these same people will go out all day and come back with nothing. As in any shopping situation there will be items which represent good value and others which you would be better off purchasing at home.

- **WHY ARE SOME OF THE PRICES SIMILAR?**

With the introduction of the internet and instant access to all sorts of commercial information the traditional European bargain is slowly disappearing. The world is becoming smaller, and the shipment of goods from one place to another more frequent and more substantial. So that a levelling process is under way, shifting the emphasis of the shopper from the old-fashioned bargain to name-branded products exclusive to a particular country. Among these particular items there are still bargains to be had of course because you are dealing with the countries which are home to many of the designer label products. I have had people mention to me that some products they could buy for similar prices in their own countries, however on further investigation it was revealed that many of these products had been made under license in order to be priced competitively.

However under all or any of these circumstances it pays to remember one thing. As a rule, you will usually only get what you pay for.

- **IF YOU SEE IT AND LIKE IT, THEN JUST BUY IT, AS YOU MAY NOT SEE IT AGAIN.**

As the traveller moves through each country he or she will encounter all sorts of one-off items exclusive to that particular place. In Italy, for example, it might be high quality clothing produced by a local company and distributed within a small selection of designer stores. Also large department stores in major cities such as Florence or Venice will have a great selection of designer labels to choose from. So if you like it buy it because you may not see these exact items outside of Italy or the home country in which they are produced.

In Paris for example shops dealing in antiques and objects of art are prolific around the vicinity of the Louvre museum and old books are to be had in the Latin Quarter. Paris is also a great place to find exquisite gifts and lingerie. So grasp the opportunity of purchasing anything that takes your fancy at these places while the opportunity is there.

In Spain Lladro porcelain and Toledo swords might claim your attention.

In Italy it will be worked 18 carat gold of some kind. There will also be Tuscan leather, wonderful Italian wines, glassware from Venice, and Italian silks.

Austria is famous for its hand-made and hand-painted glass, and for cleverly carved wooden pieces. But be aware of customs regulations and what you can and can't take back to your own country. Swarovski crystal from Austria is famous around the world and much of it is highly collectable.

In Germany there is designer clothing exclusive to that country and among the most popular souvenirs there are cuckoo clocks, beer steins, Solingen knives, ceramic figurines such as hummel and goebel as well as the worlds famous steiff teddy bears and other animals and not to forget painted pewter ware.

In Switzerland watches are the thing to buy, the extent of the watch industry there being quite mind-blowing.

Holland is famous for its diamond trade, and ceramics, porcelain, and tulip bulbs are also popular purchases.

Czechoslovakia is known for its puppets and art and like most European cities handles a large volume of antiques through its innumerable outlets.

Hungary has exclusive herrend porcelain, lace and linen and many famous wines especially the well known king of wines and wine of kings the 'tokay'.

The list is endless throughout Europe. There is just so much exclusive merchandise in each country you visit. When it comes time for shopping your tour director will usually point you in the right direction. Just let them know your wants.

- **WHAT'S BEST TO BUY.**

A lot of this boils down to what you want. Discuss your interests with the tour director because they are the people most likely to have the kind of information you require. They might have been involved in the tour industry for some years and have had the opportunity to compare prices from one place to another. They will also generally know where to source various items. So tap into their experience. That's what they are there for.

If you rely on your own judgment in such situations you might be disappointed. You arrive in a country that is new to you. You probably don't speak the language. You have no idea of the pricing structure, or whether or not you are going to be treated fairly. So don't hesitate to take advice from someone who knows the ropes.

Over the years we have found that a lot of people have enjoyed picking up Swiss watches. There are several advantages here. The price is usually moderate.

128

The quality of each item is unquestionable providing you are purchasing from an authorized dealer and as you go about wearing and looking at the item day in and day out for the rest of your life you'll be constantly reminded of the great time you had on your European holiday.

Many famous brand-name German knives are worth considering too. They will usually have a lifetime guarantee and cost as little as half of what you might expect to pay for them back home in your own country.

Something to watch out for is the trade in replicas, fakes and counterfeit items in Europe. Most brand-name articles of wide repute will often suffer from this problem where unscrupulous operators will make and sell illegal copies of the product to cash in on its good name. The price of these items will generally be lower than the real thing, and the quality a lot lower. So always buy from a reputable and authorized establishment to be sure of getting the genuine article. Another less known aspect of street trading is that some of the stalls can be fronts for questionable activities in the background.

In Italy you might like to obtain a good pair of designer sunglasses. These can be world-class but the best place to buy them is on one of the large city opticians where you will be spoiled for choice and after-service. Sourcing them elsewhere is not always a good idea.

• BUYING AT MARKETS.

A lot of tourists will head for the street markets because they believe that is where the bargains are. Others enjoy haggling over the prices at these places and the whole experience can sometimes be more important to them than any purchases made. Which is fair enough.

But I'm not a great fan of buying at markets because I don't believe you can always get realistic value for money at these places. If you are looking for a quality product and do not find what you are looking for in a recommended store or flagship store of a designer product, I always suggest to have a look in one of the large local department stores just as you would at home, you will find that the quality should be good and pricing should also be fair.

Don't rely on any warranties or guarantees you might be given at a street market. These people can sometimes be here today and gone tomorrow, their assurances and promises therefore being unreliable, for example I once bought a pair of shoes at a market which fell apart on the day I bought them. Back at the market the trader gave all sorts of reasons why he couldn't refund my money so I chalked the incident up to experience.

It's the old story of let the buyer beware. Because often when trying to shop on the cheap things have a habit of becoming a life experience in what not to do again in the future. So be wary, and remember "caveat emptor".

On the other hand, if you are shopping at markets and really know your stuff you can sometimes do very well.

I heard the story of a chap who purchased a diamond in the Grand Bazaar at Istanbul. He paid $US 5000 for it much to the horror of the people he was travelling with who were convinced that he had been done.

But when he had the diamond valued in another country it was found to be worth five times what he paid for it, the secret being that he knew his subject.

- ## DUTY FREE SHOPPING FOR TOURISTS.

As an international traveller you are entitled to duty free shopping around Europe and even in your own country before you leave as well.

In Europe there is a large network of outlets which offer a service known as 'Global Refund'. www.globalrefund.com When purchasing from any of these outlets be sure to ask for a tax refund form. It's important to know that what is involved here is not a discount but a true tax refund which in places like Italy can run out at about 15% of the purchase price if the cost of the article is above a certain pre-set limit. Establishments which don't offer the tax refund facility may try to offer clients a 10% reduction instead if they are paying by cash.

However the tax refund is in addition to any other discount you may be offered, so don't confuse the two. A lot of the trading concerns mentioned in tour company brochures will often ask the tourist making a purchase whether or not they qualify for a refund because of the fact they might be about to take the goods out of the country. They know that ninety nine percent of the time customers will be doing this so will have the facilities on hand to issue the appropriate paper work. Your tour director will be able to explain to you just how the system works.

Usually when you are about to leave the last European Union country the procedure is to present the goods along with your passport and the refund form which will be stamped by customs officers and the refund may sometimes be given at the airport or be re-credited to a credit card.

- ## POSTING IT HOME INSTEAD OF CARRYING IT.

Many large European trading establishments will offer a shipping service through which larger items can be sent home. Some consider the charges for this sort of thing to be a little high but these costs need to be considered against the inconvenience of carting the goods around for however many days the tour or your holiday has yet to run.

Take care when packing fragile items. Do it yourself or supervise anyone else who has offered to do it for you. Don't buy chocolate and send it home or carry it around for days, especially in the summer. Chocolate does not travel well so eat it soon after purchase.

- ## THE BEST WAY TO PAY.

I always tell my clients that the best way of paying for purchases is with a credit card. And there are three good reasons for this. First, having a card saves you carrying around substantial amount of cash. Second, some credit card companies will give you insurance of one kind or another for items obtained with their card. And third, paying with a card gives you some degree of comeback should your purchase prove unsatisfactory in some way.

Your first purchases in a foreign country.

Shopping in a foreign land can be a lot of fun. There is the challenge of a different culture, you might have difficulty communicating your needs to the assistant because of language problems, and the whole exercise can be quite time-consuming. The thing to remember is to wear a smile at all times and the person you are dealing with will generally help you to the best of their ability.

- **YOU HAVE READ THE BOOK, YOU HAVE SEEN THE MOVIE, NOW YOU GET TO MEET THE PLAYERS.**

Most travellers have read a book on the country they intend visiting. Or maybe they've seen a movie set in some place which has further strengthened their resolve to visit that particular country. Now suddenly they are going to be in those places they saw in the movie and meet the people who may have been extras in it so to speak. They saw meals which looked fantastic on the television but the real thing isn't necessarily going to measure up to their expectation. There may be too much garlic. They might serve your favourite dish cold when back home you always have it hot. But it was fantastic nevertheless, reading the book, seeing the movie and meeting the players even though some things in real life were a little different from what you expected.

- BUYING YOUR FIRST COFFEE. I ONLY WANTED A COFFEE BUT I GOT AN AMERICAN BREAKFAST.

These comments are based on an experience I had in Paris while setting out to meet a colleague of mine. Along the way it started to rain so as I was in the area I ducked into the Ritz Hotel. When I spoke to reception I asked them if it was O.K. if I could have a cup of coffee. They agreed, and I was directed through to the breakfast room and duly seated. I indicated I wanted a coffee and sat reading a paper while waiting. I gazed around the room and couldn't help noticing how nice everything looked. Someone asked if I would like an orange juice, or a fruit salad, it all looked so good I decided to accept the offer and continued sitting there for another thirty minutes or so.

When it came time to leave I was given the bill and saw that I was being charged for what they called an 'American' breakfast. I imagined the coffee, fruit salad and juice I had was going to be about 5 or 6 euro but was floored to discover that it was actually 45 euro. When I had time to regain my composure I realized that what they had indeed charged me for was an American breakfast and not just the items individually. Waiting staff had just assumed I was a guest, and that I'd had a full breakfast. I could in fact have had an omelet, or bacon, or cheese and bread, or anything else I fancied but whether I had eaten these things or not I was being charged for them. This procedure was hotel policy.

The whole episode was a bit of a shock at the time but it has turned into a nice little story which I hope will benefit others. It wasn't worth getting bent out of shape for. There weren't thousands of dollars at stake. It has become an interesting memory and one I've shared with many, many people over the years.

• SOME OF THE MOST DELICIOUS ICE CREAM I'VE EVER EATEN, AND WHY DID IT COST SO MUCH?

The ice cream stories have been passed back to me over the years by clients who also received a shock when it came time to pay for something. In this case ice cream.

The people were asked to pay 6 euro for two scoops of ice cream in Venice and what they didn't realize is that if they had taken their purchase off the premises the price for the same ice cream would have been only about 2 euro. Sitting down in the café where they bought it attracted what is known as a 'restaurant' price.

- ## SOME OF THE MOST EXPENSIVE COFFEES – PIAZZA SAN MARCO AND THE HOTEL DANIELI.

When you are ordering something from the counter in any major European city quite often the attendant may say 'sit down. I'll bring that to you'. You may be ordering a coke and a pizza, and be thinking to yourself that it's only going to cost you about 10 euro. Next thing a knife and fork and napkin arrives, and a little basket of bread, your coke comes in a glass, and your pizza on a plate, and when you get the bill you may find that instead of the 10 euro you were expecting, you now owe 20 to 25 euro. The reason for this apparent high amount is that you were given a 'sit down' meal which included cover and service charges.

In some European countries you are charged 10 euro just to sit at a table. I know that in the Piazza San Marco if you have a couple of people having a drink and listening to the music and a third person comes along – one of their friends maybe – and sits down with them, despite the fact that the newcomer hasn't even ordered a drink, they will be given a bill just for taking up space and listening to the music. The philosophy being that if that person **hadn't** been sitting there, another who might possibly have bought a drink would have. Hence the venue might have been able to make more money.

So be prepared for this type of thing. They aren't actually rip-offs. The locals know and accept them. It's just that they are unfamiliar to visitors from other lands who go home and tell their friends about the shock they received.

There is a difference between being ripped off and not being aware of the reasoning behind some of the seemingly exorbitant charges. As far as I am concerned, being ripped off is when extra drinks are added to your bill, or extra dishes added to the meal you just had. Was it a mistake? Or was this purposely done? And if so, does it happen every night? You have to wonder. Because when they are caught the offenders usually apologize profusely, they simply can't believe it happened, and they're sorry. And people go away from the place almost feeling sorry for the waiter. 'It was so bizarre', they tell their friends. 'They made this mistake and were so apologetic'.

I've seen many venues throughout the world consistently make the same 'mistake'. Sometimes the scam is picked up on. Sometimes not. If you are serving twenty tables in a night and 'accidentally' charge two extra drinks to each table and you get picked up on it say, seventy percent of the time, you are still going to net 50 or 60 extra dollars or euro per evening. So always **check** the bill wherever you are.

5

ON THE TOUR

The first day talk.

- AN ABBREVIATED LAYOUT.

Personal Intro: Welcome to previous clients – brief history – congratulations on choosing this tour – I have set aside the following number of days to run the tour – you are the most important people to here so whatever you need make sure you speak with me – if it's important to you it's important to me – point out codes and emergency phone numbers – please listen – it's important what we are about to talk about – much of the information your travel agents would have told you – however for those of you who didn't receive much information you may find the following interesting ...

- BREAKDOWN SCENARIO.

The Tours: A tour is a relationship between people. The key to a successful tour is to be easygoing and relaxed.   The holiday – the movie syndrome.   You will notice there are no queues in the movies – enjoyment of the tour largely comes down to the individual. How much you get out of the tour will largely depend on how you adapt to the differences. There are many different tours run by many different types of companies. I will explain some of the main differences.

THIS IS A TOUR OF EUROPE STAYING IN HOTELS, NOT A TOUR OF EUROPEAN HOTELS.

Arrivals: Please stay on coach till we check in.   I will give room numbers.

The hotels: Air conditioning coming to Europe soon.
1   European hotels and rating systems are different to your own countries.
2   Hotels will vary from country to country.   Swiss hotels are not like Italian hotels. And vice versa.
3   Our hotels guarantee us a bed and a shower and a place to leave our bags.   They represent excellent value for money due to company purchasing power.
4   Some hotels are central – some are unique – some are modern. Each has its own benefits.
5   Some hotels outside the city centre are better value for money.   Offering more spacious rooms and a

more comfortable nights sleep , they are less likely to be noisy and more likely to be air-conditioned.

6   Porterage if included – is normally one bag per person – Please don't bring your bags down yourself.

7   There are often no tea and coffee making facilities in the hotel rooms.

8   Hotel laundry – sometimes it's cheaper to buy new clothes.

9   Mini bars in rooms will sometimes be locked and reception will require a credit card security deposit before opening.

10 On rare occasions the brochured hotel may change.

11 Outside phone lines may be locked until credit card security deposit is given.

12 Some hotel lifts are small and slow so allow plenty of time to get to the coach for an on time departure.

13 Room sizes can vary. As outlined triple twins and singles.

Triples: Rooms are not necessarily larger than doubles or twins - only there are more beds – sometimes you may have to look for your bed. It may be delivered to your room after check in.

Twins: Get used to two single beds in one frame – some European countries don't distinguish between twin and double.

Singles: Smaller rooms designed specifically for single habitation. You are mainly paying for the privacy and not having to share a bathroom with anyone.

Room Mates. Generally with companies that offer a room mate matching service, you will find that rooms are non smoking. And while all efforts are made to find a suitable match there are no guarantees.

- HOTEL FACILITIES:

Reception: Normally English is not their first language – service can sometimes be slower than you expect – they may provide local information, maps, postage, money exchange available at most but not always and rates are suitable for the convenience provided.

Safety Deposit Boxes: There may be a limited amount at reception. If you are given a key to a hotel box make sure you do not lose it as some of these can be costly to replace. If using safety deposit boxes in your rooms make sure they are bolted in. Also a good idea is to have a couple of trial runs before you place any valuables in them just in case they lock up and you cannot retrieve your valuables.

Keys: Some of these can be costly to replace if lost. Anywhere from 10 to 20 euro each – get in the habit of handing them in every time you leave.

Phones: Sometimes very costly – get friends to call you – some hotels will also charge you for making reverse charge calls.

Bars: Hotel bars are sometimes costly – often there are no regular opening times – depends on business – please do not take your own drinks into hotel bars.

Any Charges: Please settle any accounts the night before or twenty minutes before breakfast.

Tour Information sheet: Usually will be located near reception – or the lifts – sometimes you may have to hunt around for it.

Wake up calls: Rely on them only for backup – **IT IS BEST PRACTICE TO BUY AN ALARM.**

Outside laundry service: Very scarce – become your own laundry – handwash small items try to pack some quick dry clothes – irons are hard to come by – try steaming alternatively consider purchasing an iron between 3 or 4 couples.

Situation: See reception first for keys, locks and towels – if they fail to help then ask reception to contact me – for locating people ask reception they will have a room list - remember things may take longer because of language problems so smile and be nice.

Room parties: Use your head – no outside guests – don't souvenir from your room – be discreet – be security conscious.

Meals: Simple meals catering to many tastes – continental breakfast may consist of – croissants, rolls, butter, jam, tea and coffee and juice and sometimes cereal – no matter how good it looks do not wrap it in a napkin and take it for a lunch snack. Lunch is at your own expense. Dinner is a basic three course – soups, salads or pastas may be a first course followed by mains of pork, beef, fish or chicken then finishing with dessert.

At dinner: Please be on time and dress appropriately. Your tour director and driver may not sit with you. Different companies have different policies, if this is the policy of the company you are travelling with don't feel offended. If you have a question feel free to ask.

Overall: The hotels are a place to sleep and put your bags – we don't spend a great deal of time in them – they are good value for money – just look at the back of the door – compare the nightly hotel rate with the cost of the tour per day.

Departures: Coach won't leave until …
- All bills are paid.
- All keys are returned to reception – check your rooms thoroughly before departure as it is very expensive to retrieve any items that may have been left behind.

Health/Hygiene:
1 Don't get worn down.
2 Purchase some fruit daily (whatever is in season).
3 Get multivitamin tablets.
4 Most drinking water in European countries is fine to drink if not sure, ask.
5 Rest when you need to.
6 If you feel unwell see a doctor or pharmacist and get the necessary medication ASAP.

Security:
1 Passport t/c credit cards. Should always be in your money belt.
2 Personal security.   Be aware of people in your personal space.
3 Coach security. Leave nothing on the coach that if lost or stolen will hinder the continuation of your tour, i.e. passports, travellers cheques, cash, medication etc. The coaches should always be locked when unattended but this is no guarantee of security.
4 Don't leave valuables in hotel rooms.

5   Lock doors in hotel rooms. When sleeping this is standard business travel practice.
6   Don't leave valuables under your mattress.
7   Watch out in crowds. This is when you are most vulnerable to pickpockets.

In Coach:
1   Practice tolerance many different wants from many different people.
2   Have a considerate and easygoing attitude.
3   Some companies have a seat rotation policy in order to give as many people as possible the opportunity to experience touring from many angles.
4   Different areas of the coach will be warmer and cooler depending on the location of air conditioning units and coach engines as well as sunlight through the windows.
5   For your comfort place a sweater between your head and the window if sleeping.
6   It is best to avoid bringing food onto the coaches for many reasons. You will normally make plenty of stops and have time to eat then.
7   It is appreciated by your fellow travellers if you remove any rubbish from your seat area so that the next day it is clean for them to sit there.
8   Should your coach be restroom equipped exercise caution when moving around the coach.
9   Don't place any heavy items such as bottles or large cameras in overhead racks on the coaches as sometimes these may dislodge and cause injury.
10 Familiarize yourself with any relevant emergency procedures.

Tour logistics:

1 Tour time – is different from normal time – what it means is there is one tour and one me and this tour follows one path as designed in the brochure from which you purchased the tour.
2 Early mornings – late nights.
3 Europe is big approximately the same size as Australia and the USA.
4 Service stops are generally made every 2-3 hours depending on traffic.
5 Service stops – why they differ around Europe.
6 Toilets – how much to pay.
7 When crossing borders, please do not take photos or videos and keep the isles of the coach clear for customs officers should they board the coach.

Drugs:
NO DRUGS ON TOUR.

Differences:

1 Europe has been around for a thousand years.
2 No better, no worse – it's just different.
3 Language, food, currency – be patient – don't lose you sense of humour.
4 RHS of road – don't get flat.
5 European culture and tradition 3000 years old – it won't change for us.
6 Siestas, church dress, weekends are all different.
7 Closures are out of our control.
8 Tipping, guides, waiter service industry, etc.

Tour director:

1 Talking lots so please be quiet – respect the people around you.
2 My first concern is the group – I have set this time aside for you and your enjoyment is my main priority.
3 Approachable.
4 Not a tour guide but a tour director.
5 Day sheets – organize times and meals.
6 Can't dance, sing or stand on my head.
7 Endeavour to tell you what's interesting.
8 Situation solving is part of my job – I am here to take the hassle out of your holiday.

Tour Driver:

1 Get us from A to B safely.
2 Do his best with your assistance to keep the coach clean.
3 Coach free day.
4 Driving regulations.

How the tour runs:

1 Tour is organized to show you as much as possible in your chosen time frame.
2 This is achieved by combining the tour which you purchased from the brochure and the optionals available at the time of the season in which this tour operates.
3 We endeavour to blend the various types of time to achieve the most successful touring experience.
4 We only have one coach and we only have one tour director.

5   Travel days begin approximately 7.30am and conclude approximately 5.00pm.
6   Sometimes stopping to visit cities en route and other times just driving direct from one major city to another.
7   Most driving is on motorway/freeway/highway due to restrictions imposed on secondary road systems.
8   We will normally stop every 2 ½ to 3 hours.
9   What is included – sightseeing.
10 What is highlight – program or excursions.
11 What about free time? Use it, don't waste it.

What breaks a tour:
1   Small independent groups forming.
2   Negativity – generally from over expectation – consistent complaining – people come away to relax, not to listen to whinging.
3   Competing with each other.
4   Not being punctual.
5   Security, and being robbed.
6   Not bringing enough money to enjoy what's on tour.

Money:
1   Budgeting.
2   Take plenty.
3   Basic costs.
4   Account for souvenirs.
5   People take one of two courses. Which one will you take?
6   I am an expert in spending money – I am not here to help you save but spend and get the best experiences and value – there is a big difference.

What makes a tour:

1   Remembering you booked a group tour – getting involved – joining in.
2   Accepting that things will be different.
3   Experiencing as much as possible – foods – drinks – museums – sights.
4   Understanding why things are not the same as home.
5   Don't have too high an expectation.
6   Treating people how you would like to be treated yourself.
7   Please and thank you – showing your appreciation.
8   Most importantly, relax.

Summary and Conclusion:

1   This tour should be a success.
2   You chose to be here.
3   Seeing some of the best countries – trying some of the most amazing foods.
4   Opportunity to have a great time with great friends.
5   Respect each other's decisions and the reasons they are here.
6   I am here to look after you so make sure you speak to me for whatever reason you need to.
7   Your satisfaction is paramount to me and as mentioned, I have the most at stake on this tour.

THIS TOUR IS TO BE THE HOLIDAY OF A LIFETIME FOR YOU. WE GIVE YOU THE PAINT AND THE CANVAS BUT YOU WILL DETERMINE THE PICTURE YOU LEAVE WITH.

> ***Please remember at all times that my first priority is your enjoyment, and if it is important to you then it is important to me. Thank you all for your attention and have a great tour.***

The Tour Director.

The tour director should be your most valuable ally while on holiday. They have the most to gain by filling this role, and the most to lose if they don't. If you are satisfied with the product, i.e. the tour and the efforts of the tour leader, they have the most to gain because if you are asked to fill in a survey by their company, and the survey results are good, that tour director will get more work. If the traveller feels he or she has been treated well, and has received excellent service, the director also stands a very good chance or earning an extra tip and therefore their income is going to rise.

Tour Directors have the most to lose in that if neither of the above are satisfactory they will not be given the volume of work by the Company they are contracted to, and income from tips will be down as well.

Do understand that anything your tour director tells you is in your best interests and is largely designed to generate the best outcome for the group. They are not doing it for themselves. The tour director's income will depend most on the traveller's level of enjoyment and satisfaction throughout the tour. Remember that at all times the customer is the one who has the last say and this is why the tour director will go out of his way to look after him/her to the best of their ability.

- **WHO ARE THEY?**

Tour directors hail from many different lands. Some are European. Some Canadian, American, Australian and New Zealanders. They may come from literally all over the world.

- **WHY DO THEY DO IT?**

Tour directors will relish this kind of job because they enjoy meeting people, they enjoy travel, and they enjoy the excitement of sharing what they know with others.

- **WHAT'S IN IT FOR THEM?**

As mentioned above, they have much to lose and much to gain. For that reason they have had to become more professional in order to maintain a continuing high level of service, and thus a higher income.

- **IS IT A CAREER?**

Tour directing is very much a career. Some people might wonder about all the time directors spend away from home but the remuneration package offered by some companies makes the job attractive enough to put up with this sacrifice. And if the clients on the various tours are appreciative of your efforts it can become more rewarding still. Total remuneration is not over the top when compared with other employment opportunities. For anyone considering taking on tour directing as a career the pay package could best be described as being in the 'middle income' bracket if you are good at what you do and the season is reasonable, or alternatively in the lower end of the income bracket if the season is slow and numbers are down. It is definitely a career which is largely affected by trends and what is popular at the time. So if you need regular stable income, you may wish to consider a different career.

- **HOW DO I BECOME ONE?**

Various educational facilities will offer training courses or else you can apply directly to a tour company either in your own county or in Europe. There are many things to learn but if you are sincerely interested in meeting people and travel then it can be an exciting and fun learning curve.

Getting along with people.

This chapter is about getting along with people you meet along the way. It is important to understand that whether making a request or a complaint you know what the people you are dealing with may be thinking. And this understanding can be a crucial factor in the outcome of the discussion. I will not claim to be an expert at this sort of thing. Nor that during my career everything has been smooth sailing. But I will say that when I have put into practice the principles outlined here I achieved what I felt was a better outcome than had I not utilized these tools of negotiation.

Open your discussion with a smile and use your body language in a receptive way rather than in a defensive or aggressive way. If you appear friendly and willing to compromise, and you show the other party that you understand their point of view, and can empathize with them, then you are close to getting what you want, or at least being listened to when you want to express your point of view.

Always mention something you have enjoyed or are pleased with before making a request or constructive criticism. Make clear what the problem or situation is that needs to be approached and give as much information as possible.

I once had a client who told me they needed to see a dentist yet when I offered to arrange an appointment they informed me that they did not have the money to pay for the visit and would I not go as far as making an appointment. Several days later the subject came up again and on offering to make an appointment I was told once again not to bother. It was not until the following day I was informed that the reason for the visit to the dentist was to obtain antibiotics. Had I known this on the first day I could have obtained them in the first couple of days.

What the tour involves.

- ## THE FIRST DAY TALK. PREPARING YOU FOR THE TOUR.

At the beginning of the tour, or just about any life experience, one of the most important things is to be prepared. You are already on the tour your travel agent promised would be the trip of a lifetime, despite the fact that he or she may not have done the particular tour you chose, or any tour for that matter. So it's a little bit difficult to start preparing now. However do not despair because the 'first day talk' delivered by the tour director will help you get rid of all your preconceived ideas and enable you to begin with a clean slate. They well and truly prepare you for what lies ahead.

The first day talk will generally put you at your ease about the decision you have made to travel with a group. It will cover many subjects and provide you with a lot of valuable information. The director will introduce themselves and give a brief description of their own travel experiences and some of the highlights of their career so far. Sounding very much like a resumé to an employer your tour leading is sharing this information hoping to establish their credentials with the group and hopefully to allow them to begin building their trust in them, this trust being an important component in the effective running of any tour. Because if the group does not trust and have confidence in their tour director various travellers will not feel happy about the decision they have made in purchasing their tour. And if they are not happy with their decision they will find it very difficult to enjoy their holiday.

• WHY IS THE FIRST DAY TALK DONE ON THE FIRST DAY?

Much of the reason for providing the first day talk on the first day is to anticipate likely questions that may arise during the course of the tour. The reason for doing this is that I have found that most of the frustration of people travelling to a new area is caused by lack of knowledge. They weren't given any explanations, and therefore lacked understanding of why different things happened in a different way in different countries.

The first day talk is designed to fix that problem, because I have found that if most of the potential questions can be dealt with in the earliest part of the tour, any grief likely to manifest itself will quickly be alleviated.

There are many examples I could give but one of the easiest to explain is what we call the concept of 'Austrian' beds. This is where it is not unusual to walk into your hotel room and find what first appears to be a double bed, despite the fact that the room had been booked by two single travellers. If this situation has not been previously explained to them many people will immediately go to reception and complain about the fact that their room only has one bed in it. People to who the matter has been explained know that all they have to do is pull don the top sheet to reveal two single mattresses which have been made up as individual sleeping areas. A double size spread is thrown over both beds.

I have known of tours where the principle had not been explained beforehand and within moments of arriving, large numbers of people were to be seen at reception complaining that they had been given the wrong room. Imagine now the person at reception trying to explain the matter in a language which is not their native tongue to a tired and confused tourist who has just sat through several hours of information from their tour director on how best to enjoy their holiday in Europe – but they left out the bit about Austrian beds.

The Austrian bed situation is just one of many matters which need to be explained on the first day as it alleviates any problems. If this is not done situations will begin to arise on the second and third day which could have been avoided. Such things as people being late, or luggage not being placed outside rooms at appropriate times for luggage collection, or people having trouble changing money, or people looking for friends in the hotel and not being able to find them, or people not adhering to seat rotation even though it might be a policy of the tour group a person is in, and so on.

When all these things have been explained to people beforehand group touring can be a great success. But if the tour director begins talking about the events after they have occurred problems can arise. For example, if they raise the late luggage situation where people may not have put their luggage out on time, some people could take it personally. When the tour director begins to explain the importance of these things the people who put their luggage out late may feel they are being got at. That you are talking about them specifically. So they feel they have been embarrassed in front of the group and suddenly for no real reason will decide you have taken a dislike to them because their luggage was put out late. Therefore they are now going to take a dislike to you because you embarrassed them in front of the group. And so it goes. The seeds of disharmony have been sown, and although the above incident sounds unusual, it isn't. These things can and do happen.

So for the benefit of both the tour participants and the tour directors this talk is best done on the first day in order to avoid any confusion from the outset.

THE TOURIST PRAYER

Oh heavenly father, look down on us your humble obedient servants, doomed to travel this earth taking photographs, mailing postcards and walking around in drip dry underwear.

We beseech thee of Jesus to see that our plane is not hijacked, our luggage not lost and that our overweight baggage goes unnoticed.

Protect us from unscrupulous taxi drivers, porters and unlicensed English speaking guides.

Give us this day, divine guidance in the selection of our hotels, that we may find our reservations honoured, our rooms made up and hot water in the taps.

We pray that the telephone works and that operators somewhere speak English and that there is no mail waiting for us from loved ones needing money.

Lead us oh God to good inexpensive restaurants where the food is good, the waiters are friendly and the wine is included in the price.

Give us the wisdom to tip correctly in currencies we don't understand and forgive us for undertipping out of ignorance and overtipping out of fear.

Make the natives love us for what we are and not for what worldy goods we can bring them.

Give us the strength to visit the museums, cathedrals, palaces and castles listed as a must in the guide books. And if perchance we take a nap after lunch or skip an historic monument, have mercy on us for our flesh is weak.

Please God, keep our wives from spending sprees and protect them from bargains they do not need nor can afford. Lead them not in to temptation for they know not what they do.

Almighty father keep our husbands from looking at foreign women and comparing them to us. Save them from making a fool of themselves in cafes and nightclubs. Above all do not forgive them their trespasses for they know exactly what they do.

And when our travels are over and we return to our loved ones, grant us the favour that someone will look at our videos and listen to our stories so that our lives as tourist will not have been in vain.

AMEN

TRAVELLER'S CODE

1   Thou shalt not expect to find things as they are at home for thou left home to find different things.

2   Thou shalt not take things too seriously for a carefree mind is the beginning of a carefree holiday.

3   Thou should not let other tourists get on thy nerves as we are all here for the same reason and thou art paying good money to enjoy thyself.

4   Thou must know at all times where thy passport lies, for a man without a passport is a man without a country.

5   Thou shalt not worry, for he that worrieth, hath no pleasure. Few things are fatal.

6   Remember thou art a guest in other lands and he that treateth his host with respect in turn will be respected. To learn to speaketh please and thank you in thy hosts tongue will make thee thy hosts friend.

7   Thou shalt not judge the entire people of a country by one person who was a poor host.

8   Thou shalt remember to err is human and to forgive is divine.

9   When in Rome, thou shalt be prepared to do as the Romans do.

10   Thou shouldest remember that if thou was expected to stay in one place, thou would have been created with roots.

SOME USEFUL PHRASES

ENGLISH	FRENCH	GERMAN	ITALIAN	SPANISH
Good Morning	Bonjour	Guten Morgen	Buon giorno	Buenos dias
Good Day	Bonjour	Guten Tag	Buon giorno	Buenos dias
Good Evening	Bonsoir	Guten Abend	Buona sera	Buenos tardes
Good Night	Bonne nuit	Gute Nacht	Buona notte	Buenos noches
Hello	Bonjour	Hallo	Ciao	Hola
Goodbye	Au revoir Auf	Wiedersehen	Arrivederci	Adios
Thank You	Merci beaucoup	Danke schoen	Mille Grazie	Gracias
Please	S'il vous plait	Bitte schoen	Per favore	Por favor
Your Welcome	Je vous en prie	Bitte	Prego	Denada
Yes	Oui	Ja	Si	Si
No	Non	Nein	No	No
Excuse me	Excusez-moi	Entschuldigen sie	Mi Scusi	Perdoneme
My name is..	Je m'appelle..	Mein Name ist..	Mi chiamo..	Me Llamo..
How are you? usted?	Ca va?	Wie gehts?	Come sta?	Como esta
Do you speak...	Parlez-vous...	Sprechen sie...	Lei parla...	Habla usted...
English?	Anglais?	Englisch?	Inglese?	Ingles?
I don't understand	Je ne comprends pas Francais	Ich verstehe kein Deutsch	Non Capisco Italiano	No comprendo Espanyol
Little/Small	peu/petit	bisschen/klein	poco/piccolo	poquito/pequeno
Big/Good	grand/bien	gross/gute	grande/bene	grande/bueno
Where is.....?	Ou est....?	Wo ist...?	Dov'e...?	Donde esta...?
Toilet	les toilettes	die Toilette	il gabinetto	los servicios
Bank	la banque	die Bank	la banca	un banco
Chemist	une pharmacie	eine Apotheke	una farmacia	la farmacia
Post Office	la poste	das Postamt	il postale	el correo
Taxi	taxi	ein Taxi	stazione di taxi	la estacion de taxi
Train	Le train	der Zug	il treno	el tren
I would like..	Je voudrais...	Ich haette gerne	Vorrei..	Quisiera..
How much is..?	C'est Combien?	Wieviel kostet?	Quanto costa?	Cuanto cuesta?
The Bill	l'addition	die Rechnung	il conto	la cuenta
Stamp	Timbre Grammatesimo	die Briefmarke	Francobollo	Sello
Ladies	Dames	Damen	Donne	Senoras
Gentlemen	Messieurs	Herren	Uomini	Senores
Open	Ouvert	Geoeffnet	Aperto	Abierto
Closed	Ferme	Geschlossen	Chiuso	Cerrado

One/Two	Un/Deux	Eins/Zwei	Uno/Due	Uno/Due
Three/Four	Trois/Quatre	Drei/Vier	Tre/Quattro	Tres/Cuatro
Five/Six	Cinq/Six	Fuenf/Sechs	Cinque/Sei	Cinco/Seis
Seven/Eight	Sept/Huit	Sieben/Acht	Sette/Otto	Siete/Ocho
Nine/Ten	Neuf/Dix	Neun/Zehn	Nove/Dieci	Nueve/Diez
Water	Eau	Wasser	Acqua	Agua
Still/Sparkling	natural/mineral	Stilles/Sprudel	naturale/con gas	sin/con gas
Coffee	Café	Kaffee	Caffe	Café
Tea	The	Tee	Te	Te
Milk	Lait	Milch	Latte	Leche
Beer	Biere	Bier	Birra	Cerveza
White Wine	Vin blanc	Weisswein	Vino bianco	Vino blanco
Red Wine	Vin rouge	Rotwein	Vino rosso	Vino rojo
Bottle	une bouteille dedie	Flasche	Una botiglia di	una bottella de
Glass	un verre de	das Glas	Un bicchiere di	un vaso de
Ice	Glace	Eis	Ghiaccio	Hielo
Hot	Chaud	Heiss	Caldo	Caliente
Cold	Froid	Kalt	Freddo	Frio
Cheers!	Sante!	Prost!	Salute!	Salud!
Meat/Fish	Viande/Poisson	Fleisch/Fisch	Carne/Pesce	Carne/Pescado
Seafood	Fruit de mer		Frutti di Mare	
Vegetables/Chicken	Legumes/Poulet	Gemuese/Haehnchen	Verdure/Pollo	Verduras/Pollo
Fruit	Fruit	Obst	Frutta	Fruta
Bread/Butter	Pain/Beurre	Brot/Butter	Pane/Burro	Pan/Mantequilla

Complaints.

'No one told us there would be fish in the sea. The children were startled'.

'We had to queue outside with no air-conditioning'.

'It's your duty as a tour operator to advise us of noisy or unruly guests before we travel'.

'The brochure stated "no hairdressers at the accommodation". My friend and I are hairdressers. Will it be O.K for us to stay there?'.

'It took us nine hours to fly to Jamaica from England yet it only took the Americans three hours.'

'I was bitten by a mosquito. No one said they could bite'.

'We booked an excursion to the water park but no one told us we had to bring our swimming costumes and towels'.

'We found the sand was not like the sand in the brochure. Your brochure shows the sand as yellow, but it was white'.

'I compared the size of our one bedroom apartment to our friends' three bedroom apartment and our was significantly smaller'.

'There were too many Spanish people in Spain. The receptionist spoke Spanish – the food is Spanish – too many foreigners'.

The foregoing is a sample of some of the various complaints that have been generated through the travel industry. The reason for including them is to provide a little humour before you travel. They may also give you a bit of an insight into what some of the people in the industry may have had their lives shaped by, and the events that may have made them who they are today.

So if you think your tour guide is very laid back and sometimes doesn't react in a panic to what may be seen as an absolutely disastrous situation such as a vehicle accident, or a client falling, or even being run over, the reason they look so relaxed is that their brain has gone into problem-solving mode, rather than panic or stress. This enables them to resolve the situation faster, and to ensure the continued smooth running of the tour.

I remember a tour I once conducted for an 18 to 35 age group, a large proportion of which were heavy drinkers. Normally on one of these tours with 50 or so people there will be half a dozen or so who will drink in the bars on a nightly basis. However on this tour the nucleus of the drinking group was around 35 people, which was an unusually large number.

The unique thing about these people was that they were a very polite and a nicely spoken mixture of males and females who just found they got on extremely well together. But unfortunately, the heavy drinking took quite a toll on their numbers and on this particular tour I would have seem more hospitals than in the previous three or four years.

However to isolate one incident, a young girl on the tour was dancing the Greek Zorbas with several other members of the group in one of the stopover bars. Now if you are familiar with the Zorbas you will be aware that it moves in a sideways fashion. This young lady happened to be on the end of the dance line holding a wine glass in her left hand while having her right arm around another member of the group. It was then during one of the sideways movements that the young girl tripped and fell sideways to her left, with some of the rest of the group falling with her. Unfortunately, when falling, she put her left hand which was holding the glass out to break her fall and subsequently fell on the wine glass. This happened more or less right in front of me and when I stepped forward to help her up I noticed that she had fallen on the wine glass and it had gone into her neck leaving a very large wound that was bleeding profusely.

I immediately covered the wound and then set about assuring the girl that she was going to be O.K. and that we needed her to relax while we got someone else to have a look at the situation and make a decision about what needed to be done next.

Meanwhile we had already called for an ambulance to come to the venue and despite it being reasonably late in the evening we also informed our local agents who over the years have always been of great assistance in cases of emergency. Many people will know who I am talking about and I know will agree with what I am saying. We will call them the magnificent Florentines. But back to the story.

Fortunately on this particular tour one of our party happened to be a doctor and was kind enough to offer her opinion.

By now however we suspected that the ambulance was no closer than when first called and that more immediate action was called for. So we put the young lady into a vehicle and took her to Casualty, or Pronto Soccorso, as it is known in Italy. Also at the hospital to offer his assistance was my friend a colleague Paolo.

The patient was admitted and the doctors treated her immediately. She began complaining of having no feeling in one of her lower arms and of having trouble moving it. Medical staff had little to say at first then quickly suggested she be moved to a specialist facility where she would be able to receive a much more detailed examination.

I returned at this point to the accommodation and began writing up a detailed report of the night's events as per Company requirements.

Then after no more than a couple of hours sleep I had to escort the rest of the tour group into the city of Florence for their day of sightseeing. My day developed into a combination of running between the hospital, the accommodation, and the city and then in the evening the hospital, the restaurant, and the nightclub where the group was having an evening out.

I was ably assisted by my driver Mark through all this drama and I owe him a huge vote of thanks, not only for what had just happened, but also for helping me on a previous occasion as well. One night in Hopfgarten he helped take my mind off a rather uncomfortable situation which required surgery the following day. It is amazing how good a painkiller schnapps is. If the Austrian doctor had been around I'm sure I would have let him perform the operation while I was standing at the bar if he'd asked me.

By now I had been able to snatch only about two hours sleep over the last thirty six. We eventually found out that the young lady would be unable to continue her tour and that both herself and a friend would be terminating their European holiday in Florence. So I would need to inform her parents of the situation and continue with the tour.

Two more hours sleep and we were on our way to Rome. Over sixty hours my total sleep was still only about four or five while ensuring that everyone was looked after.

This situation happened several years ago and for sometime I kept in touch with the young lady to find out how the rehabilitation of her arm was coming along. I did in fact speak to her only this year and was informed that she is now married and working in France where thing are going well for her.

Now all this said, if you see a situation unfold in front of you such as someone falling over, or a person who has been robbed or pickpocketed, or injured in traffic, and wonder why your tour leader is not getting frantic or starting to panic, you need to know that it is not because they are not emotional, or do not have empathy or feelings. It is because as part of their job as a tour director and group leader, or as the person who has to make sure that everything is done as efficiently as possible, they must maintain a cool head. They must first assess the situation and then act to ensure that everyone is taken care of to the best of their ability. And also, that any third parties which need to be involved are contacted and then lastly, when everyone else is taken care of, they will stop to think about themselves. Yet while it would be appreciated, they do not always expect to be thanked.

Because think about it. Would you want to be treated by a doctor who fainted at the sight of blood?

By the same token, you don't want a tour director who cries the minute something goes wrong.

Differences.

- TOILETS: AS MUCH AS YOU MAY WANT TO YOU DO NOT HAVE TO SPEAK TO THEM.

There are so many different bathroom and toilet facilities you come across while travelling you could almost write an entire book solely on this subject alone. In a nutshell, some of these are operated on sensors so that as you leave the cubicle the cistern flushes automatically. At others you need to look on the floor for a button which is depressed with your foot. And some have self-cleaning mechanisms which cause the seat to rotate and clean itself before you actually use it. The same with some hand basins. They too can sometimes be equipped with sensors which activate self-cleaning mechanisms. Some are activated by a lever or button on the floor also operated with the foot. Still others will have a button on the wall to cause the water to flow.

- **WHY DO WE PAY FOR THE TOILET AND HOW MUCH SHOULD IT COST? AND WHAT HAS BEEN THE EFFECT OF THE EURO?**

This has to do with toilet facilities once again. The introduction of the euro as a universal currency throughout Europe has had the effect of pushing up prices. In Italy before its introduction the charge to enter a washroom was 200 lira, which equates to about 10 euro cents. But this has now risen in a lot of cases to 50 euro cents.

These conveniences need regular cleaning and upkeep and in western countries both the supply of water and labour is not cheap. Hence the widespread implementation by local authorities of the user pay philosophy.

With most of the washroom facilities throughout Europe there is an entry charge, so be prepared with a few coins in your purse or pocket. There are a few free ones of course but they are not necessarily well maintained. Within Europe the average charge to enter one of these facilities is between 20 and 50 euro cents. At some places the attendant takes the small change from the cash bowl and leaves one and two euro pieces, the idea of this being to give the perception that previous visitors have all paid one or two euro each. But in many of the facilities unless it is in fact sign-posted with the official cost the correct procedure is to donate between 20 and 50 euro cents.

- **SOMETIMES YOU REALLY WOULD BE BETTER OFF HEADING FOR THE BUSHES.**

That's right. Especially when the facilities on offer don't really measure up however this is quite a rare occasion. In Italy and other places, most of the service stop facilities on the main highways within Europe as well as heavily frequented facilities you will find they are generally in good order.

- **WHY NOT MANY OF THE LOCALS DO.**

You'll notice sometimes that some of the locals will not contribute towards washroom expenses for one reason or another. Some will of course, but they are exceptions. Different countries will often have different arrangements in this area – with differing results, you'll notice.

- ## THE VIOLENT FRAUS, AND LOO TRICKS FROM COUNTRY TO COUNTRY. HOW DO THEY GET YOU TO PAY MORE?

In some countries, signs in some wash facilities will be written in a foreign language but no two are run in exactly the same manner. In some the attendant will allow you to use whatever it is you want to use before you pay. In others the attendant might not be so forgiving and despite the sweat on your brow and crossing of legs while you still try to walk, will insist on not letting you past until you've paid your money. Once again, the old trick of only having one and two euro coins on hand has the effect of separating the travelling public from their small change.

In Britain in areas of major transport concentrations such as Charing Cross Station, or Victoria Station, bathroom facilities are on a user-pays basis too, the approximate entry fee being 20 English pence. Entry is regulated by way of a turnstile mechanism.

Some people new to the idea can't seem to accept tipping as a custom but if they were to add up all the money they spent on bathrooms during their tour they'd find that it could easily amount to 2 euro per day. Because the money is going out a little at a time it's easy to overlook the fact that you are spending so much.

- ## WHAT IS THE MEANING OF THE WORD 'DOUCHE', AND WHY DOES IT COST 2 EURO?

In some toilet facilities in France there will sometimes be seen a sign which states: 'Douche, 2 euro'. Foreigners have walked in assuming that 'douche' meant 'bathroom' or 'wash facility' (or a weird assortment of other strange things) and thought they were being asked to pay 2 euro to use a toilet or bathroom. Douche of course means wash or bathe and these particular facilities are there more for the use of heavy vehicle drivers who may be staying at a nearby service stop and were in the habit of taking a shower before driving on.

- ## LANGUAGE, FOOD AND CURRENCY. TRY NOT TO LOSE YOUR SENSE OF HUMOUR.

I usually say to people that the most difficult obstacles to negotiate on a tour are those which revolve around language, food and currency. If you have a basic understanding of these three thing then you're half way there.

You can soon acquire a limited grasp of a language, even if you just learn a few words such as 'hello', 'good-bye', or 'thank you'.

Quite often people will order different types of food and not always get what they asked for. For example, despite the fact that many places will advertise an American-style hotdog the fact is I doubt whether such a thing exists in Europe.

Currency has become much easier now with the introduction of the euro to many European countries but dealing with totally different coins and notes can take a bit of getting used to for some.

The important thing to remember is that no matter what obstacles you do come across try to handle them patiently and with some humour. As long as the incident didn't result in the loss of thousands of euro (or dollars) to you you'll find that you will have an interesting story to tell your friends when you get back home.

- **THE CULTURE OF YOUR CHOSEN COUNTRY IS PROBABLY MANY HUNDREDS, AND EVEN THOUSANDS OF YEARS OLD. DON'T TRY TO CHANGE IT.**

One of the biggest things to remember with any of the countries you are travelling through is that their culture is likely to be many hundreds, or possibly thousands of years old. Don't try to change it. To do so is almost like trying to re-invent the wheel.

- **SIESTAS:**

Siestas involve the closing down of many mainstream commercial activities between approximately mid-day and four o'clock. Some visitors find this a little bit odd but remember it is part of the tradition and culture of the place. Lunch is often taken as the largest meal of the day and children will even go home from school to have a rest, or a sleep. This slow down takes place to avoid the hottest part of the day when temperatures in southern Europe can exceed 40° Celsius.

An interesting thing about siestas is that quite often in many counties telephone rates will be cheaper during siesta hours because most of the heavy commercial users will be home having a sleep.

• CHURCH DRESS:

In many of the predominantly Catholic European countries church attendance means that you come along suitably dressed. Suitable in this context meaning that you have your knees and shoulders covered. For gentlemen the preferred dress is some form of long trousers and a conventional shirt or a polo shirt with a collar, for ladies, the general rule is not to wear provocative clothing such as clothing which leaves you midsection exposed, and once again have your knees and shoulders covered. Some churches are more lenient than others, the most strict being St. Peter's church in Rome where they have a very firm policy of no entry if your knees or shoulders are showing. Also, it is not advisable to carry back-packs or bags into St. Peter's, or for that matter, any of the principal museums throughout Europe either. You'll need to check your bags in at a cloakroom area and collect them again later when you exit the building.

It is also not allowed to take any sharp items into museums and art galleries, such items as scissors, corkscrews, Swiss army knives have become objects of fear and mistrust since September 11th, and are liable to confiscation.

- WEEKENDS:

Visitors to Europe will often have a hard time understanding Continental weekends because there is not always consistency from one country to another. Sometimes shops will be open on a Saturday or a Sunday but close on Monday to compensate. This is particularly so in Italy or Holland so don't assume that a particular day will be an ordinary trading day just because it is back home.

- TIPPING:

You'll find that for the different countries you are visiting there are different systems for, and different levels of, tips and tipping, or what is referred to universally as a 'service charge'.

The tour director will advise what the recommended amounts are in each country and there is much literature written on the subject.

A general rule with tipping is that if you believe you have had excellent service then you'll leave an excellent tip. If you believe you have had good service you will leave a good tip. And if you believe you have had no service then you will leave no tip.

Transport systems.

- BUYING BUS TICKETS:

There is a choice of many different transport systems throughout Europe, depending on your preference.

Whether it be a bus system, or underground, or metro, or rapid transit, or taxi, all have their advantages and disadvantages.

With the bus system you can either purchase single trip bus tickets for one person, right up to block bus tickets or day trip bus tickets. The most important thing though is to ensure that any tickets you do but are validated properly before entering the transport system. Transport authorities in Europe and elsewhere no longer accept unfamiliarity with the transport system as an excuse either for not having purchased proper tickets or for not validating tickets. Not getting it right can result in a fine large enough to spoil your holiday.

So be familiar with the systems you are going to use to avoid crossing over to the wrong side of the law.

- BUYING TRAIN TICKETS:

Much the same requirements and penalties apply to the purchase of train tickets.

- TAXIS IN FRANCE, ITALY, GERMANY, SPAIN, SWITZERLAND, AUSTRIA, ENGLAND, HUNGARY AND THE CZECH REPUBLIC.

When it comes to taxis in the different countries around Europe be aware that different cities have different regulations. As mentioned in an earlier chapter, countries such as France will generally only allow three people in a cab at any one time. If there are more than three people in your party you will either need to pay a supplement or else order a special taxi through a special company.

The Italian taxi service is similarly structured. Except that you will need to pay a boundary charge if the taxi you have hired needs to travel beyond its normal operating boundaries. So be aware that if you are being picked up from some of the airports around Italy you'll need to pay that charge.

Stories abound regarding the creativity of some Italian taxi drivers. We hear about how they take people on circuitous scenic tours instead of going straight to the hotel, and then charge plenty. But in my experience using taxis in Italy, most of the time they have been very, very good, and a lot of the stories about their unscrupulous behaviour can be unwarranted. So once again, be prepared. Know approximately how much you should be paying, agree on a fare with the driver if you can, and thus avoid any unnecessary problems later.

If you are travelling by taxi from Chartes de Gaulle airport to the centre of Paris you could quite easily pay 40 euro for the trip. In Italy, a comparable journey from the Leonardo da vinci or Fiumicino airport to the centre of Rome could cost anywhere from 35 to 45 euro depending on traffic conditions.

Germany has quite a tightly regulated taxi system for its fleets of largely BMW and Mercedes vehicles.

Spain has a very efficient taxi system, and in Switzerland, hiring a cab can be quite expensive. This country has one of the highest living standards in the world so do be prepared to pay for that. Austria generally has a good taxi service.

In England the drivers of the traditional black cabs are regarded as the most professional in the world. It takes them up to three and a half years in order to gain their taxi licence, and there are other areas of study they need to master too.

In tandem with the conventional taxi fleets in England are the mini-cab companies, but you would be advised to familiarize yourself with these before you use them. Some of them operate quite unprofessionally, and it is best to approach a particular firm only on the recommendation of someone who has used it several times in the past. But with English taxis generally you will get a very professional service and a novel ride in a traditional vehicle.

The taxi service in Hungary can vary greatly from one city to another, and from one company to another, with some firms being a bit more reputable than others. Services can be a bit hit and miss at times and as with the nearby Czech taxi service enjoys a degree of notoriety for taking people for a ride in more ways than one. Many Hungarian taxi drivers will not speak English despite the fact that many of their companies advertise an English-speaking service. The problems begin when the driver arrives and you have difficulty making yourself understood.

Meeting the locals.

'I want to meet the locals', we hear you say sometimes. Meeting the locals when you're travelling just about anywhere in the world has taken on a whole different meaning over the years due to the fact that many counties have become very global and very international. Therefore you can find that the novelty for the locals to meet someone from a different country has quite possibly worn off a little. Most of the major cities will be similar to cities in your own country, where the citizens are too busy working their fifty or sixty hours a week just to keep their job, and don't have a lot of time to spend with their local friends or even their families without going out of their way to introduce themselves to foreigners, and offer them free guided tours around the city.

Meeting the locals may have been a lot different twenty or thirty years ago when tourism was quite a new thing. However the position has changed markedly over recent years. If you are determined to mix with locals it is probably best to do it in the smaller towns or country areas where the pace of life is a lot slower, and where meeting strangers is still a bit of a novelty. There is a downside to this however. These days people can be a bit wary about being approached by strangers who suddenly start talking and asking things. Also unfortunately in the past some people have done this and taken advantage of the villagers by taking advantage of their hospitality in one way or another. So meeting the locals has to be handled tactfully, and as mentioned, the smaller country towns are generally the easier places to do this.

Motorway service stops. How they work.

Service stops are strategically situated along most main highways throughout Europe for the comfort and sustenance of travellers. They sell food and drink and sometimes films and CD's but of most importance to some, all have full washroom facilities available for between 20 and 50 euro cents.

FRANCE: Most famous stops here are known as L'arche. Upon entering one of them you will notice two or three different areas you can use. There is the takeaway section where you can buy coffee, croissants, baguettes, fruit, etc. And there is a self-service, light meal facility where the food is always fresh and the choice of items on sale quite bewildering at times.

The Italian Auto Grill network is also beginning to gain a foot-hold in France and operates along similar lines to L'arche. The cost of a light meal at either place is around 10 and 12 euro or you can pay by credit card. More substantial a la carte facilities are also available but it is not recommended to use these unless you have a lot of time to spare.

At the stops there is also a washroom section where 20 or 30 euro cents will buy all you require.

Telephones are available for the public also.

ITALY: Stops in Italy are slightly different from those in France. In some respects they are unique. When you go into the 'entrate' you will exit via the 'uschita', having progressed through the facility on a one-way system. First there is the food takeaway counter, followed by the self-service section. And finally, you will need to walk all the way through the supermarket section where you will see a vast array of cheeses, meats, wine, films, batteries and so forth. Payment for anything bought here must be made as you leave.

There is no seating at the takeaway area. Whatever you purchase you must stand and consume at tables and benches. You will notice too that the people handling the money are not the same ones who handle the food.

There are all kinds of bread available and Italy is famous for its different types of coffee. Fruit and salad bars cater for those on a health kick and pizzas, risottos and pastas round off the kinds of food you would expect to find in Italy.

Service stops are good value for money as they are always trying to encourage people to make use of their facilities. Reasonable prices reflect this goal and apply to the locals as well as to overseas tourists.

Procedures at Italian service stops are a little bit complicated, and first time visitors do sometimes find the experience a little daunting. But they can be a lot of fun, especially in the 'queues' where with head down and elbows slightly splayed you move towards the food with authority rather than aggression. Everyone is playing the same game. They are all abiding by the same rules. So don't be intimidated. Just get in there and go for it. If the whole thing is still too much for you ask the tour director for assistance.

SPAIN: With service stops in Spain I can only wish you 'good luck', and advise that you always keep your sense of humour at the ready. The system of queueing is much the same as in Italy. In other words, there is no system.

Spanish service stops vary greatly from one place to another but the ordering and paying for food and drink is much more simplified than in France or Italy.

The Spanish like lashings of garlic on much of their food and many different type of tortilla are available. A wide variety of sausages and all kinds of cheese give the traveller many choices. The Spanish also do nice legs of lamb and fish dishes presented in a variety of sauces. In winter there are hot soups heavily flavoured with garlic while in the hot summer months a cold tomato soup called gaspacho is very popular. Latin desserts are quite simple affairs by comparison. Finger foods and many fine wines round off the offering.

AUSTRIA: The Rosenberger service stops in Austria are incredibly efficient, are visually appealing and have a very professional air about them. No matter how many people there may be in the facility they are handled efficiently and with expertise. Unlike some other countries, the emphasis here is not so much on takeaways but more on a gift shop–type setup where you can buy drinks and sweets and even small souvenirs.

There is a self-service area where you can pick up such things as bread, cheeses, cakes, soups, pasta dishes, fresh vegetable, and different meats and fish dishes as well as beautiful goulash and stews. As well as these items there is a large range of different coffees available.

Many tour companies will use Rosenberger service stops because doing so is a very efficient use of time.

GERMANY: In Germany there are many different types of service stops but as in most places there is the usual self-service, takeaway and cafeteria section in each one. They range from excellent to very basic.

If you are wishing to use the bathroom at these stops keep your eye open as you enter the building for a sign which says 'W.C' or else a picture on the wall of a man and woman pointing downstairs. If you are a disabled traveller you will find that many of the better stops have a lift system for your convenience.

HOLLAND: Throughout the Netherlands a good network of service stops cater for the traveller, with all the usual dining and washroom facilities. They are not nearly as crowded as those in Italy or France.

SWITZERLAND: The Movenpick chain of service stops here is an efficient network of facilities similar to those in Austria. Movenpick are also well known for their ice cream.

Travel security.

- ## WHY HAND BAGGAGE IS CALLED HAND BAGGAGE.

Hand baggage or hand luggage is so called because the luggage is on the end of your arm and that's where is should always stay. When you are travelling you should never put it down for even a minute due to the fact that it is small and likely to contain the most important documents and most valuable items you have with you. For these reasons it can be the prize target of thieves and bandits.

To you it might be another piece of luggage which is a nuisance to carry but to the thief it contains the best of everything, i.e. purses, wallets, passports, credit cards, cash, digital cameras and small expensive gifts. And I am sure that if you did a quick calculation at any point of time on your holiday you would see that the cost of replacing all the items in your hand luggage could run into several thousand dollars (or euro). Let alone the inconvenience. So never put your hand luggage down, or leave it even for a moment, or take your eyes off it for any reason.

- ## HOW LONG HAVE YOU KNOWN THE PERSON YOU JUST ASKED TO WATCH YOUR LUGGAGE?

We all like to feel we are reasonable judges of character. But something that has always interested me is how after knowing someone for not much more than a few minutes we will ask them to watch our luggage or personal belongings for us. Especially when there are large numbers of people present. Good examples of this situation is when people are waiting at airports or train stations and need to go to the bathroom and don't want to drag their baggage with them into a cubicle.

- **DON'T WORRY. THE LOCALS GET RIPPED OFF TOO.**

I remember once I was at a Hungarian street party where a small café was selling beer for 300ft which is the equivalent of just over one euro for a half litre. But the problem was that they were only filling the glass up just over half in many cases and it was only if you pointed this out to them that they would bother to top up the glass. Now I watched them pour about twenty glasses in this fashion to both locals and tourists alike and only a small percentage of these people pointed out the lack of beer to the barman. Most people just looked at the glass with a degree of disappointment, shrugged their shoulders, and walked off.

So just remember that in many of the big cities traders are blatantly indiscriminate. They don't really care where the money is coming from just as long as it comes.

Pickpockets.

Around the world pickpocketing can be a very lucrative form of income for those who indulge in this sort of activity. While travelling in Europe it is quite common to hear horror stories about it and while extremely annoying pickpocketing and deception generally are not seen as violent crimes. Usually you won't even notice that your belongings have been pilfered until you next go to use them.

The simplest form of pickpocketing is when people approach you and ask for change, or money, and while they are distracting you in this manner their friend will go around to the other side of you and lift your purse or wallet in a flash from your bag or pocket. And you won't feel a thing. Sometimes they will present you with a map and ask for directions, all the while holding the map over your bag, or your backpack if you are sitting down at a café, and while you are looking at the map will reach into your bag and deftly remove something from it before calmly walking away.

There is also what is known as the old 'throw the baby' trick, sometimes used by the nomadic populations in the Latin country busy city locations where somebody acts as though they are about to throw a baby at you, because they are faking a stumble over a crack in the pavement, and you are handy, so they are looking to you to save the child. You drop your bag in alarm and an accomplice appears from nowhere and snatches it up before disappearing into the crowd. You are left holding the baby – literally.

There are many different methods of pickpocketing and deception. I always advise people never to advertise the fact that they are carrying substantial amounts of money. Don't flash it about. Don't pull out a large wad of notes in public to pay for a small purchase. Be discreet. Professional thieves only need a quick glance at your open wallet to get a pretty good idea how much cash you are carrying. You are always being watched by people who mean you no good.

I put it to people this way. If you could earn 500 euro a day tax free would it sound like a tempting job? And of course most people say 'yes'. That's exactly what pickpocketing can be like for some dishonest people. It's a career choice for them.

If someone like this has noticed you are carrying a large amount of money they will literally follow you for the entire day waiting for you to put your bag down, perhaps at a fast food outlet, and when you throw your bag or pack temporarily over your shoulder while carrying the tray of food to a table, they will come along behind you, unzip your bag, and next thing your money is gone and so are they.

At bathrooms and washrooms you may put your bag on the floor while using the facility and the thief goes along looking under the doors of the cubicles and snatches up whatever they can. They usually make good with their escape because it is very hard chasing anyone with your trousers down around your ankles.

So these are just a few of the things to be on guard for when travelling. Other things to be on guard for are people offering flowers in piazzas, or city squares. You will select a note from a number you may have and say 'is this enough?' The person offering the flower might then snatch the largest note or notes they can see and then run off. You're left holding a flower which may have cost you 20 euro or more. So do be aware as you travel around that some people might see you as the golden goose.

In many parts of Europe pickpocketing and other forms of deception are seen as soft crimes, and as there is no physical injury associated with them they are not heavily over-regulated or policed.

The best way of guarding against these 'soft' crimes is not to let anyone intrude into your personal space, be wary in crowded or confined areas such as crowded buses or trains, be aware of where your belongings are when getting in and out of vehicles, and most importantly, have a money belt which can be placed below a layer of your clothing. All you really need to carry each day is a credit card and maybe around 50 euro in cash to pay for incidentals.

I often say to people that moving through a city is a bit like bear hunting. The most important thing you need to take when you go bear hunting is someone who runs slower than yourself. When it comes to pickpocketing and security follow the following golden rule and that is to make sure you are a harder target than the people surrounding you and you'll probably be left alone.

Taking your photos.

When on tour it is always a good idea to find someone in your own group who shares the same passion as you do about photography. That way, when you need to enlist the aid of someone else to take your photograph in front of a place like the Eiffel Tower for example they'll pay more attention to composition and the like than someone who doesn't know much about the subject. Or who isn't interested. In return you can offer to do the same for them when the need arises.

- ## WHERE TO TAKE YOUR PHOTOS.

While travelling be sure to have your picture taken in front of major tourist sights. People later will then be able to very easily recognize where you went on your tour. As well as that, if you were to have a photograph of yourself taken in front of places like the Eiffel Tower in Paris, or the Arc de Triumph, or a bullring in Spain, or the Leaning Tower of Pisa in Italy, or a dozen other famous monuments and landmarks in Central Europe, when you get back home you can have the best of them enlarged and framed and placed on the wall in a conspicuous part of your house where friends and relatives can see and talk about them. The display will make a great conversation piece, and you'll be able to share memories with people who may have been to the places depicted, or else you can whet the appetite of those who haven't been.

But don't be like some people and put your photographs away in a cupboard or drawer where they mightn't be seen for a long time. The whole idea of these moments captured on paper is to jog the memory and remind you of the good times you had and the people you met. So don't hide them.

- ## GETTING THEM DEVELOPED AND KEEPING A RECORD.

Sometimes people will snap away quite feverishly over the course of a tour and not keep an accurate record of what or who they have taken photographs of. If other people are in some of the pictures it's very easy to forget their names later. You may even forget the name of a town, or even a country where some of the snapshots were taken. This spoils the value of each one so to prevent this kind of thing it's a good idea to keep some kind of a record of all the relevant little facts as you go along. Jot them down in the journal at the back of this book. And do it roll by roll if you have a film roll camera.

For those with digital cameras, and because aspects of the technology are still largely untested and unknown, print off the most important photos as soon as you get home.

Something else that many people don't consider is that when you have twelve or fifteen rolls of exposed film ready to process, money can be saved by obtaining quotes for the work. You can approach specialist photographic shops or go straight to the big city pharmacies which usually have a photographic department. Competitive prices can be obtained in this way.

- ## THE BENEFITS OF GOOD PHOTOS.

There are a number of benefits attached to having a set of good holiday photos. You have a good record of how you spent your holiday. You can enlarge the best of them and hang them on the wall at home. If some are of particular excellence you may wish to enter them into photographic exhibitions or submit them to travel magazines for possible publication. Some may be good enough to mass-produce postcards from.

- ## THE GROUP PHOTO.

There are a number of things to consider in respect of the group photograph. If a group photo is offered by all means avail yourself of the opportunity because it might be the only chance you get. The cost will only be about ten or fifteen euro which is good value for money.
If a professional photographer is involved they will generally know how to arrange the group to get the best shot where everyone can be clearly seen. They will put the taller ones in the background and the more petite people up front. Most likely they will arrange them in five or six short rows with about a metre to a metre and a half gap between each row. And finally, they will take

up an elevated position in front of the group so that they are slightly looking down on everyone. The result should be a photographic study to remember, especially if taken against a famous and recognizable background.

Sometimes the effect of the group photo can be enhanced if everyone turns slightly toward the centre of the group. The area of ground required for the photo can be compressed and quite often people are shown up in their best light when this happens. (makes you look a bit thinner too if you have been enjoying the cuisine a little.)

At the time the photograph is taken it's a good idea to make a list of all the people in it. There's no way you are going to remember all their names a year or two down the track.

Tipping

- **THE HISTORY OF TIPPING:**

Tradition has it that tipping had its origins on the trading floor at Lloyds of London. In a nearby café traders would meet to discuss business and when one of them was ready to place a trade they would leave a coin on the edge of the table. Eventually this would be spotted by a runner who automatically knew what to do. Pocketing the coin, he would collect the trade and run it to the floor. Hence the word 'tips' – To Insure Prompt Service.

• WHY DO WE TIP?

Many people have had the experience of dining out at a restaurant where the surroundings were clean and elegant, the food top class, but the service itself was absolutely terrible.

You're seated at a good quality eating house which came highly recommended, you've heard so much about the exquisite food, and now you are expecting a night to remember.

But what happens?

The waiter or waitress doesn't appear to be taking any interest in you. They are not very prompt serving you. Twenty minutes go by before you can place a drink order. The meal comes to the table late and cold. There is no apology. You feel you are not being looked after. You are not being made to feel important. You wonder whether you are a burden to the staff rather than a guest. And your night to remember will be exactly that but for all the wrong reasons and soon the stage is reached where you feel you would rather be some place else.

It's really a question of service. Or in the circumstances just outlined, a complete lack of service. And this is important in the hospitality industry. A good product plus good service equals a successful business. A business can hang or fall on the level of service its employees provide because this is the one thing patrons remember and talk about. It's the service which brings them back to a particular restaurant – or drives them away. They want to go back because they were made to feel special. Or they might never want to go back because of the sub-standard way they were treated. The service might have been practically non-existent.

And this service principle doesn't just apply to restaurants. Tour directors, coach drivers, guides, taxi proprietors, porters and other people encountered on a tour all provide a service of one kind or another. And the quality of that service can vary.

If you found that a tour director, for instance, didn't treat you well, or was not pleasant, or maybe wasn't even very good at his/her job, you might start feeling that you weren't getting what you paid for. So you would feel inclined not to reward that person as well as someone who might have provided a much better service, and who made your holiday a fantastic one instead of just average.

And so to reward good service it has become common practice throughout much of the world to show your appreciation by paying a cash gratuity. For excellent service you pay an excellent tip. For average service you pay an average tip. And for poor or no service you don't pay any tip at all. And this system ensures the survival of people who are good in the industry. It also weeds out those who are not so good. And since tipping can form a substantial part of a person's income their continued survival in that job depends heavily on the type of service they provide. Excellent service means they are assured of an adequate income. Poor service means a low intake of tips and a consequent dramatic dip in income. Hence the eventual exit of these people from the industry altogether.

Some sectors of the hotel or food industry will only pay their bar people or serving staff a token hourly rate.

And since these workers may need five or six hundred dollars a week to live on the remainder of their income must come from tipping.

Some businesses in the hospitality industry will pay no wage at all. They will actually charge people wanting to work for them. Some well known eating houses are patronized by people known to be very good tippers so that there is stiff competition among service staff to gain a position at such establishments. At these venues you may have to pay the employer a levy in order to compete for the privilege of working there.

Some tour companies have a similar policy whereby tour directors actually purchase clients from them in the hope of obtaining a good level of tipping later on. In this way talented and professional directors maintain a good level of income while those not providing an acceptable level of service are soon forced to seek employment opportunities elsewhere.

So that's why we tip. It's a tangible way of expressing our appreciation to the people who have provided us with a high level of service and created an experience to remember rather than a painful memory you just want to forget.

- ## WHEN DO WE TIP?

Quite simply we tip once we feel we have received good service.

• WHEN DO WE NOT TIP?

When we believe we have received poor service, or no service at all.

• WHAT HAPPENS IF WE DON'T TIP?

If we don't tip, and the person who was serving us is aware of why we didn't tip, then it doesn't really matter very much.

I've been to restaurants were the service was top class but the food left a lot to be desired. That wasn't the waiting staff's fault. They did the best they could with what they had. So they got their tip however I would be reluctant to go back to that particular restaurant unless I was assured that the problem with the food quality had been resolved.

If we don't tip no one is going to hold a gun to our head and make us tip. And that's part of the reason why some people believe that it's not necessary to tip in the first place. But if at a good restaurant, or with a top notch tour company enough people don't tip, the good people in those industries are going to move on to where their services are better appreciated. And if this happens the level of service at the companies and establishments we favoured in the past will begin to slip.

So tipping is the mortar which hold the service industry together. It is a most accurate self regulating system to ensure as high as level of service as possible as we tour around from country to country. So do try to allow for tipping when working out your finances.

• WHY DO THE BEST VENUES MAKE US FEEL SO GOOD?

Basically, because the best venues or tour companies have the best staff. It's that simple. And staff at these places are the best because in a gratuity-based industry they are the best paid. If they weren't being paid what they felt they were worth they would simply move on.

Good service staff are professionals in their field because they know what they are doing. Bar staff know their wine lists backwards. Tour directors know how to extract the best out of each area visited. Restaurant waiters know what it takes to make people feel special. So this is what we are tipping for when we come under the influence of these people. We are paying for a professional service, and know-how, and for savvy.

But if after reading this you still only want to pay peanuts for any service received you'd better watch out. You might end up getting only monkeys next time, and monkeys won't necessarily make you feel good.

It takes well paid service staff to do that.

• WHY IS TIPPING NOT INCLUDED?

Because a lot of people who have already been paid have no incentive to excel themselves. Those with a poor work ethic will even say: 'why should I go harder? I've already been paid. There's no point in killing myself'.

So tipping is with-held to encourage service staff to do their very best. The level of service rises as a result

196

and the bar person or waiter can deservedly anticipate a suitable gratuity.

But there are always going to be those who won't tip. They go to venues and utilize services which are of very good quality but are shy and retiring when it comes time to pay up.

Tipping is a bit like giving blood. It might be a little painful at the time but once the process is over you feel great. You know you have done something worthwhile. Unlike those who would like to do it but can't quite get over the mental hurdle of actually carrying it through.

I always tell people once they are aware of how much tipping might be involved to take that amount of money on holiday with them and look on it as insurance, or a purchase on their trip. By taking an extra four or five percent over and above the cost of the tour they will be guaranteed the time of their life. By not taking the extra money no guarantees can be given. The result could be a nightmare of some kind, or at the very least a serious lack of enjoyment.

Be proud of what you give to people such as tour directors and coach drivers. The amount should be fair and accurate reflection of what you feel they have done for you. See yourself as an employer of that person, and act accordingly. Excellent effort over the duration of the tour will have qualified him/her for an excellent gratuity. But if you feel they have given only half the service they should have then give them only half the suggested amount. And likewise, if the service provider has given no service at all then give them nothing. They only get back what they put in.

- ## TIPPING ON A STRETCHED BUDGET.

A sincere 'thank you' can sometimes be more rewarding than money, especially from people in the tour group known to be working on a severely stretched budget. People in this situation react in a number of ways to their plight, from those who actively dodge the staff in the last few days of a tour, to those who are forever thanking him/her on a daily basis for various services rendered. Whatever the financial situation of a tour member, a heartfelt show of appreciation from them is always welcome. Tour directors and Tour Drivers are perceptive people who will understand how some people are placed and will usually be quite content to see these particular people enjoying themselves. It isn't always about the money.

- ## GIFTS INSTEAD OF GRATUITIES.

In the service industry there are mixed feelings about gifts instead of gratuities.

I have been given little koala bears from the South Pacific, flags from various nations, bookmarks from Japan, coffee coasters from Columbia, little Indian tea towels, and so forth. I treasure the lot. These things are fun to receive and I have had some fantastic gifts over the years, all of which I have kept.

But please understand that none of these items will pay the rent or help with any luggage restrictions encountered on tour.

• WHY GROUP COLLECTION ARE NOT SO GOOD.

At the end of a tour some well-meaning person within the group might suggest a collection for the director and/or driver but there are several reasons why this is not such a good idea. Some of these reasons are from an ethical point of view, and some from a security point of view.

I once organized a collection myself for the director and driver on a tour but soon realized it mightn't have been the right thing to do. It dawned on me that I had short-changed them and deprived them of a larger amount they would otherwise have received from the group had each member contributed directly on an individual basis.

Sometimes a person who does not want to tip will attempt to organize a collection. This way their unwillingness to participate in a direct financial way can be disguised. They feel that the act of organizing a group collection is a sufficient contribution in itself, and that there is no need for them to tip as well.

But let it be said here and now – individually and personally is the way to say 'thank you' properly.

Another consideration is one of security. After the collection there might be a considerable sum of money involved, so who is going to be responsible for it? And can the person nominated by trusted? It's a responsibility that no one should have to bear.

It has actually happened in the past that professional

criminals have gone on tours, with the group tip as one of their main targets. After spiriting the money away they then claimed that their room had been entered and the money stolen. This one fact alone is enough to make the idea of group collections unwise.

- **REMEMBER TO TIP THE DRIVER.**

This little section has bee included at the request of a friend of mine, Hank, who is a tour coach driver in Adelaide. While this book was in preparation he raised the matter of tipping the driver a number of times and I back his call one hundred per cent.

The driver is the unsung hero on a tour. They make it all physically happen. From country to country and city to city they get the big coach through safely and on time. They do a good job. So show your appreciation in a practical way by giving him a well-earned tip at the appropriate time.

- **USING THE SYSTEM TO YOUR ADVANTAGE.**

Be nice to everyone. Think of how you would like to be treated and treat others in the same way. Smiles attract smiles. A positive attitude is contagious. And you only get from the tour experience what you are prepared to put into it.

Optional tours.

With just about anything in life there is bound to be an unexpected cost if you have not read all of the documentation thoroughly. For example, when most people buy their first car they are not really aware of all the expense associated with owning a vehicle. I am sure that if everyone sat down and worked out these additional costs, i.e. fuel, insurance, taxes, depreciation, registration, servicing and maintenance there would be less people sitting with their heads in their hands every time something went wrong or a new bill or invoice associated with the running of their pride and joy arrived in the mail.

The same reasoning can be applied to many things we purchase over a lifetime but cars and houses would be stand-out examples.

However with any of these items there is generally a series of benefits which will always outweigh the cost of acquisition. And in this chapter we will explore these benefits insofar as they apply to the optional excursions available with most tour packages.

- **THE TRUTH ABOUT ADDITIONAL EXCURSIONS AND WHAT YOU REALLY NEED TO KNOW.**

There are different reasons why travel agents don't over emphasize the importance of excursion programs. These people work in a very competitive environment, the job is demanding and they are under pressure most of the time. So try to be a little sympathetic.

1   Some agents don't feel confident enough to offer useful information about excursions. They are perhaps not sure what the tour company might be currently offering, or what the costs might be to the client, so they give out only what they are sure of.

2   Some agents may feel that the potential customer is cash-strapped enough without going into detail about excursions. Even though many of them are going to be highlights of the tour.

3   Unfortunately, many peoples' decisions are driven by cost rather than service. Travel agents are no different. Working on very tight margins in order to compete with companies doing business on the Internet they will want to make their travel products as competitive and as attractive as possible. And this may sometimes involve not providing information about optionals, the reason being they don't want to handle anything they are not responsible for selling or providing service for.

    With travel packages you can get anything you want if you have the money. But for most people cost is an important factor in deciding what product to purchase. And this is the reason some agents get forced down this path of trying to harmonize desires with the money available.

4   Travel agents do not have a crystal ball and are not mind readers so therefore they cannot tell what you already do and do not know. Therefore if you do not

ask about such things they will not see the point of bringing them up. You need to remember that an underlying principle of business is that time is money.

5 Some travel agents may simply not know what optional excursions are available when asked. And when you think of the enormous variety of products available at any one agency you can understand why. The deals are revised and updated each year and great volumes of specials announced on an almost daily basis and arriving constantly by either fax, e-mail or telex have to be absorbed by the agent immediately for potential customers coming in that day. It's a wonder that the uniform they wear is not equipped with several buckles and wraparound sleeves because I know some of them feel they are heading that way by the end of a tough week.

6 Most tour operators will make a mention of the fact that optional excursions are not included but will usually not go as far as to provide a comprehensive list as to what may be available either. And there are reasons for this. What may actually be on offer when you are touring may be unique for that time of the year and therefore only applicable to your particular tour. Because of peculiarities and restrictions of this kind it is not cost effective to compile information specific to each and every tour on offer.

7 If you are looking for further information regarding excursions and their cost you will find that many of the tour operators will have a website you can visit. Some of these have discussion forums at which you

are welcome to input or request information. However a word of warning. When reading discussion forum information try not to take too much notice of any negative information, as quite often this form of open discussion forum, which is relatively anonymous, does open itself to corruption in the form of professional complainers. These people may have a bias against one company or another, or an individual who takes a personal dislike to either a company or one of its employees may decide to use the discussion forums as a way of venting their feelings, as opposed to taking their gripe through the proper channel and dealing direct with the company itself. But you will generally find on these sites that for every negative comment there are around ten positive ones in favour of the company in question and its products.

8   Many people wonder if the companies make money from the optional excursions and simply put from a business perspective the answer would have to be 'yes, they do'. And so does every person you pay money to for various services every day of your life. So the tour companies make a profit because that's what companies are supposed to do. If they didn't make a profit they would soon fold and the consumer would be the loser. Just try organizing and implementing an excursion on your own. Could you design and deliver the product? Could you create an exciting atmosphere, including theme music and all relevant information? Would you know everything there is to know on the subject? Probably not. You

are putting up your ability and expertise against a big company with years of experience. I know who I would rather have dealing with emergencies and any or all obstacles that might arise.

- ## WHO RUNS THE EXCURSIONS?

The people who run the excursion are generally the tour companies themselves. For this reason the likelihood of receiving a much better product is greater than if you were to give your money to a local operator. You will remember the internationally branded company should anything go wrong but may well forget the contact details of these other people who will probably charge more and deprive you of any choice. And on a scale of one to ten your bargaining power with them will be essentially zero. It's a question of who has the most to lose by not looking after you. The big branded company is looking to you to return to your place of origin with glowing recommendations to your friends and family about their service. They are relying heavily on word-of-mouth advertising. The local operator on the other hand will mainly be concentrating on the logistics of working with people they have no real relationship with.

- ## WHY DO THEY OFFER EXCURSIONS?

Originally when group touring began many of the large companies sold their product as an all-inclusive program where you spent the majority of your waking hours in the company of your group of fellow travellers. This was a very efficient way of seeing plenty of Europe in a short time. Especially considering that when this style of touring was in vogue European travel for people from other Continents was just beginning and much of Europe was a bit of an unknown quantity with its combination of different languages and currencies.

However there were a couple of flaws with this method of travel. If some local excursion happened to be unavailable for some reason, due perhaps to an industrial dispute, or to adverse weather conditions, and this part of the program had to be cancelled, there was no way of refunding the unused portion of the tour fee.

Another flaw was that as people began returning to Europe for a second visit they would sometimes incorporate small private excursions of their own so paying for services in the cities concerned could not be justified. So some companies decided to structure their tours differently. They began offering the bare essentials such as coach transport, organized hotel accommodation and a reduced amount of included meals and sightseeing tours.

Due to these reductions their product now appeared to be substantially discounted when compared with other similar products on the market and so began attracting a lot more business. In order to keep up, other companies were forced to follow suit.

So nowadays we tend to find that the majority of companies operate in this way in order to satisfy the needs of the masses. And while there are still companies which operate fully inclusive tours, their market is much smaller and they work more at the top end of the market.

- ## WHERE DO THE OPTIONAL TOURS TAKE PLACE?

Generally the majority of the excursions will take place in the major cities or wherever there is a point of interest which is of specific relevance. They are available to the traveller when he or she would otherwise be having free time and experience has shown that this is when there is most interest. But the problems multiply when you try to organize it all on your own. Endless queues, complications of direction and not really knowing what you are looking for means you will only see one or two points of interest if you are lucky. But with the company doing all the work, guesswork and stress are eliminated and the end result is that you will see far more than you possibly could have by doing it alone.

- ## HOW DO THEY OPERATE?

Letting your tour director do the purchasing for you is generally the most effective use of your travel money.
Because when you think about it, it is the tour director who has the greatest interest in you having a good time. And if you are not happy having a good time and if you are not happy with the service you have received from them, the way you have been treated generally, and the recommendations they have given you, chances are at

tour's end you won't feel like tipping them the full recommended amount.

- ## WHAT GOES INTO THE PREPARATION OF AN EXCURSION PROGRAM?

Some tour directors may be allocated their tour anywhere up to seven or eight weeks before departure. And right from the start a good director will begin structuring a program and making all the relevant bookings to ensure the best possible use of the group's time. They will know how much travelling time to set aside, how much included sightseeing time, how much time for independent exploring and shopping, and how much time for excursions and rest.

They will choose the best excursions available as they aim to give you the most evenly balanced program possible to supplement the scheduled program you originally purchased from your travel agent.

In Paris, for example, excursions could take in such places as the Louvre museum, a cruise on the River Seine, a gourmet dinner in a quaint French restaurant, the glitter of a spectacular Parisian cabaret, and so forth. Or in Switzerland, a trip up one of the many world famous Swiss alps either by cable car, gondola, a unique cog railway system, or an immaculately restored historic train, or even a Swiss folklore show where you get the chance to try a traditional fondue. In other words in each city you will be given the opportunity to experience a good cross-section of the famous tourist attractions that exist in each area, always maintaining that crucial balance of time.

For a first visit to Europe by anyone these unique opportunities in each country are strongly recommended.

Something to remember when making a decision about what excursion to go on is that there should be no overlap between what you have already paid for at the beginning, and what you are now contemplating. If you are not sure, ask your tour director.

Another point to remember is that if you are going to dine several times in the one country make sure you are tasting representative sample of the cuisine that country has to offer. Some good examples are cakes which vary greatly from place to place, wines which differ similarly from region to region, and the numerous types of bread Germany is famous for. Try everything going.

• WHAT ARE THE BENEFITS TO YOU?

1 ***Most effective use of your time***: Having someone co-ordinate your sightseeing for you will allow you to utilize your time in the best possible way. You've already embraced this policy by joining up with an organized group tour. The best possible outcome is only possible by obtaining the best possible information.

2 ***So what does all this mean?***: If you wanted advice on the most suitable décor for your home you would speak to an interior designer. If you wanted advice on the most effective presentation for your garden

you would consult a landscaper. Advice about the workings of your car would have most credibility if it came from a qualified motor mechanic, and unless you were totally mad you wouldn't let any one other than a qualified surgeon take your appendix out. So if you wanted to see the sights of Europe why wouldn't you approach the experts?

3 **_Your tour director should be a professional in the field:_** You should be in the hands of a tour director who is a professional in their field. Tour directors are the people most qualified to advise you in the best use of your holiday time. They have the expertise, knowledge and resources to most effectively manage the perfect blend of your time so that you will extract the most from your European experience.

4 **_Value for money_**: When it comes to excursions you will find that if you compare like with like especially where local companies and operators are involved, the value for money offered by your tour company should be substantially weighted in your favor. This is largely due to the free trade that exists with many touring companies and the volume of people they collectively bring each year to the various service providers.

This results in many restaurants competing with each other in order to be seen as a venue of choice by tour operators, and accordingly are required to look after you the client as best as possible in order to maintain their standing in the eyes of the tour operator.

But do remember that while we consistently put a dollar value on so many things in our lives today, that value for money is not just about the physical things you got for your cash but also the overall feeling you had with things you cant put a price on such as excellent service, years of experience, organization, quality entertainment etc, and good times shared and lasting memories created all in the company of good friends.

A good example of this is when you sit for an hour in one of the beautiful piazzas of Italy sipping a refreshing glass of light fresh Italian wine or maybe enjoying a cool beer while you take a break and recharge before the next sightseeing experience. Or maybe you decide to reward your self with a freshly brewed Italian coffee and get to enjoy the fact that you are sitting maybe in one of the most famous piazzas in Italy enjoying a little la dolce vita while watching the world go by, feeling as if you are in the middle of a movie set or watching a scene from the theatre of life each scene being played out before you between each sip from your glass. When your bill arrives and you are maybe a little surprised that each drink has cost around 12 euro plus service. I always suggest to people not to think of it as an expensive drink, but to think of it more as good value live entertainment of which there was one show only and you got to not only see it , but to be in it as well.

Offered excursions will often include all transportation door to door from your hotel, gratuities for service staff where meals and drink service is involved, the services of local guides used for museum visits, all entrance and reservation fees, as well as any local or state taxes .

You will often find that in many cases where a dinner is not included as part of the program purchased from the travel agent an excursion involving a dinner may be offered.

Another benefit to you is that now you get to decide at the beginning of the tour rather than 2-3 months before the tour commenced.

Think of all the fun you will have when you have nothing else to worry about except for having fun. Share all of the flavours of Europe with like minded people and in great company. Touring is not only about seeing the sights, it is also an important social occasion. Sampling the various cuisines and enjoying traditional entertainment in some of the greatest cities in the world. A professional and a good working relationship between your tour director and driver will add volumes to your tour

Experience education, enthusiasm and efficiency expertise and excellence should be being striven for at all times by your touring team, the benefit of this to you simply cant be measured.

Some of the answers to common questions people have after the presentation of the excursion program.

• HOW DO I SECURE MY RESERVATIONS?

Most companies are prepared to accept settlement of accounts with travellers' cheques in any major currency including Euro, American, Canadian, Australian and New Zealand dollars, Swiss francs, English pounds and Japanese yen. Cash from these countries is also acceptable. As well, most companies will also be set up to handle Visa, MasterCard and American Express.

If paying by credit card the transaction will generally appear as a goods purchase which itself will have substantial benefits over a cash advance transaction. Because if you are doing things on your own you will find that some establishments will only accept cash. Alternatively, you may find that a trader's credit card terminal is not working correctly and they can't process your transaction. Therefore if you are extracting cash from automatic teller machines during your tour you may find that all the transaction charges will build up to quite a tidy sum. As well as that, most banking institutions will not give you an interest free period on cash withdrawals.

I would certainly suggest that if you have brought cash and travellers' cheques that you should use the majority of these early. But always be sure to keep the equivalent of 20 euro per day per person as an emergency fund. But try not to let the reserve fall below 100 euro in total. Because in the case of emergencies such as a lost money belt complete with credit cards and passport, or a visit to the doctor, etc, you will be surprised just how quickly you can use up 100 euro on incidental expenses such as phone calls, faxes, new passports photos if you have not brought any, taxis between hotel, police station, hospital, embassy, etc, etc.

Then what I suggest to do is to use your credit cards for all shopping purchases. One of the main reasons for this is that many credit card companies will offer a degree of insurance for any purchases made with their cards.

By maintaining the level of reserve cash you can then use this for bits and pieces such as ice creams, coffees, sandwiches, postcards and the like and if the reserve dips below 100 euro you then have time to arrange a top-up of funds if necessary.

- **I WAS TOLD EVERYTHING WAS INCLUDED.**

This situation can and does arise from time to time. Sometimes it is due to misinterpretation and other times it may be due to misinformation. Whichever you feel is the case give details to your travel agent, tour director, or the Company directly if you feel strongly enough about the matter. They may then feel it necessary to contact the agent to ensure that the product is explained more carefully in the future. Once you have done this then get on with enjoying your trip as you have now done what you can for the time being. If you don't inform the tour director or the Company then whatever you do, don't spend the rest of the tour complaining to your fellow tourists about the situation as more often than not you will be well in the minority of people who have received misinformation. And whatever you do try not to take your frustration out on your tour director personally. Put yourself in their position for a moment. They are trying to deliver to you a product that someone else and not them have made promises about. I'm sure everyone has heard the saying 'don't shoot the messenger'.

IF YOU ARE STILL UNDECIDED THEN I SUGGEST YOU READ THE NEXT FEW PAGES AND NOT ONLY WILL THESE HELP YOU MAKE UP YOUR MIND, THEY MAY ALSO CHANGE THE WAY YOU LOOK AT ANY FUTURE DECISIONS YOU MAY NEED TO MAKE.

- WHY YOU SHOULD PARTICIPATE IN AS MUCH AS POSSIBLE WHILE YOU ARE AWAY.

'Twenty years from now you will be more disappointed by the things you didn't do than the ones you did do. So throw off the bowlines. Sail away from the safe harbour. Catch the trade winds in your sails. Explore. Dream. Discover.'
- *Mark Twain.*

How true is this statement. Over the years I have run into many of my past clients who all shared one thing in common. They had no regrets about the things they did while they were away. They did not waste their time sitting around wondering and worrying about what to do and what not to do. They had adopted the philosophy that whatever was on offer they would get involved with. They would get stuck in and just do it. They would make full use of every opportunity that was being given to them. They wouldn't hang back procrastinating about what they might do.

On the other hand I have met those who went on journeys to faraway lands and didn't make the best use of their time. They didn't actually **do** anything while away. Most now have regrets and Mark Twain's words come to mind once more 'twenty years from now you will be more disappointed by the things you didn't do than by the one you did do'.

So with this in mind before you make any decision in the future about whether or not to have a go at anything, whether to decline an offer about doing or seeing anything new, remember this. You'll be amazed at how much more exciting life can be once you move off the sideline, gotten on to the field of play, and immersed yourself in the greatest sport of all – the sport of life.

So remember. Don't be a spectator, **Get Involved**.

- ## THE THINGS I WORRIED ABOUT MOST NEVER HAPPENED.

When it comes to stress in our lives most people will agree with the above statement. How often have you sat and worried about something which in the end never happened? This is also true when it comes to holidaying. Many people create a series of 'what-if' scenarios they use as excuses not to step out of the comfort zone to experience new things. I'm not advocating throwing all logical reasoning away. Only that there is nothing wrong in taking a calculated risk.

For example, several years ago while in Queenstown, New Zealand, I was give the opportunity to try bungee jumping, tandem sky diving, jet boating, white water rafting and helicopter ride all within the space of a twenty four hour period. I did not have a lot of money to spend but in the end decided it would probably be a while before I got back to that area so I had better seize the day. The calculated risk was that I was doing the bungee with the company who pioneered, the activity – A.J Hackett, and the parachute jump with a skydiver who had done over 2,500 jumps. All these activities were being offered by a large touring company with many international connections. The company had a good reputation. I trusted them. As with any activity or sport there is always an element of risk. By trusting this particular company I felt I was minimizing the risks.

However if for example I was being offered the tandem sky dive by a company which was not properly qualified or accredited and considered a good landing to be any landing you lived through, the white water rafting by a company which was not familiar with this river and had patches all over their boats and didn't supply life vests, the helicopter ride with a pilot who was flying while disqualified and had alcohol on his breath, and who was in an unfit mental state with borderline suicidal tendencies, and the bungee jump with a company which thought rope was just as good as elastic and real jumpers used rope, then the element of risk would obviously be increased, and I would have reconsidered what was being offered.

Needless to say everything went without a hitch. I liked the bungee jump so much I went straight back up and did another one. However this time by jumping backwards. It was called an 'elevator'. The jet boat ride was exhilarating, the tandem parachute jump mind-blowing and the helicopter and white water rafting unforgettable. I bought the photos, the videos and the t-shirts which came as part of the 'must-haves' - from such an action packed twenty four hours and to this day do not have one regret about the experiences I had then and which I can still enjoy today when I look back at what I did. And despite the cost being a substantial portion of my spending money, today I couldn't even tell you how much the cost was. But I can still remember the experiences as clearly as though they happened yesterday.

So think about this ....

There are people who make things happen.
There are people who watch things happen.
And there are people who sit around and wonder what happened.

When you go away, which one of these are you going to be?

If you need more convincing, think about the reasons people use for not getting involved. Perhaps you've used them yourself?

1   ***I will do it next time***: This is a valid enough reason if you know for sure there is going to be a next time. And that the attraction or activity is still going to be around.   For example, you can no longer fly Concorde because it is out of service. The leaning tower of Pisa has been closed for ten years for re-stabilizing.   And several other places have now stopped receiving visitors due to stricter security measures.

I have met so many people who went to a great destination and enjoyed it so much they swore they would go there again. But some never did. Other new and exciting destinations claimed their attention instead. They procrastinated, and I was guilty of this myself when I first began to travel. I would put off until tomorrow what I could have done today. My friend Peter of the Rose and Shamrock Irish pub located in Havelock North in the beautiful Hawkes Bay district of New Zealand describes it as 'a failure to implement'.

So seize the day and if the activity satisfies your needs in some way – don't fail to implement.

2   ***I am not really interested***:   Are you really not interested?   Or is it maybe that you just can't see what the activity has to offer? Or has it not all been properly explained to you?   Before making your decision speak with the person offering the service

for a little more information and tell them what you are interested in. They will try to determine whether there is any benefit for you and if not, they might be able to offer an alternative suggestion.

3   ***It is dangerous. Or, I am afraid to do that because of my phobia***: How do you define dangerous? Most danger is relative to the situation and many people will agree that both the perception and the reality of danger are two different things. Risk management minimizes danger. Awareness and education control danger. Being familiar with these principles gives people confidence and security in the decisions they make.

So before you avoid something because you think it is dangerous try to get as much information as possible regarding the risks involved and what precautions need to be taken to eliminate as many of those risks as possible.

4   ***I don't have the money***: Hopefully you have purchased this book early in the holiday planning process so this won't be a problem. However if it is a problem, ask yourself this question. It is that you don't have the money or that you do have it but would rather spend it on something else?

I have had clients claiming to be short of funds however I could see that there was one particular thing they really wanted to do while in Europe and having been helped along the way in my own travels and being a great believer in karma, I offered these people the chance to join in as a gesture of goodwill, on the proviso if they felt they could afford to pay at a later stage they could do so then and if not, that they try to help someone else out in the future in some way.

So if you say you don't have the money to do something and then proceed to spend 30 euro a night in the hotel bar and another 10 or 20 euro a day on cigarettes, etc, then do realize that your fellow travellers might start considering you a little odd.
Only use the 'I-don't-have-the-money' reason as a last resort.

5 _**You may be able to make more money but you will never make more time**_: Chances are if you are already sitting in a coach somewhere in Europe reading this for the first time, and point number four above is still making you think, you may wish to take up a religion if you don't already have one and begin praying for a miracle. Or alternatively, you may wish to think about the following before getting your undies in a twist. The comparisons at a comfortable budget level. Ask yourself the following questions.

6 _**How much money have you already invested?**_
   (a) Flights to and from point of departure approximately 1000 euro.
   (b) Travel insurance 100 euro.
   (c) Incidentals such as luggage, money belts, etc, 150 euro.
   (d) Accommodation before and after the tour 250-300 euro.
   (e) Tour cost (land content only) 1260 euro.
   (f) Allocated spending money assuming 50 euro per day, 750 euro.

(g) Time getting everything organized. You decide how much your time is worth.

The approximate total of 3500 euro is what you have possibly already committed. However you now realize that for an extra 500 or 600 euro or approximately 15% on top of what you have already allowed you could likely have the best fifteen days of your life.

You now have to ask yourself which of the three following categories you want to be in.
Those who ...

> *Make things happen,*
> *Watch things happen,*
> *Or sit back and in fifteen days time*
> *and wonder what happened.*

If your holiday is going to be a once in a lifetime event I would suggest that you pull out all the stops in an effort to get the extra money required. Because in years to come you will forget about the money and remember nothing but the fantastic experiences you enjoyed.

Just think back over the experiences of your own life where you may have blown the budget. It might have been a great party at home or a fantastic dinner in a top restaurant, a better model of the car you wanted, your own or a family wedding or honeymoon, a home extension, or a beautiful piece of jewellery. Chances are the initial cost may have caught you off guard. But once this was overcome you could just sit back and enjoy the moment. Many things come with a price tag in life. But good times spent with great friends, and the memories created by participating in such events are priceless.

7   *I don't want to tire myself out*:   Do you remember what Mark Twain said?   'that the things I worried about most never happened?'   Well this is a perfect example. I have seen people over the years who were concerned about being tired out so much that they participated in only a few of the offerings. But when they got to the end of the tour they found that they had much more money left over than they thought, they didn't feel tired at all – like they thought they would, and they now regretted not participating in more excursions.

The best advice I can offer in this situation is to speak with your tour leader and be honest with him about your possible need to have a break.

The tour leader will appreciate the fact that you are involving them with your decision.

Most people are so excited by all the fun they are having and the new sights they are seeing that their adrenalin keeps them from getting tired. Sometimes I have found that the people who get most tired are those not getting enough physical, mental, visual or gastronomic stimulation, and of course people who kept staying up and out well past their bedtime.

A sample itinerary.

The following is a sample itinerary as written for a leading European tour operator.

Please note; as we all know on the road, this information is only to be read as a guideline and not to be quoted as gospel. Things such as museum times, closure of roads, hotel locations and so on can change. So should you be using this guideline for your tour I hope you find it useful.

- **DAY ONE:**

London to Brussels – Sunday – Hotel Holiday Inn, Garden Court.

05.15: Arrive departure centre – meet driver – do final checks for tour and turn on mobile phone exchange phone numbers with driver and depart for pickups.

1st

2nd

3rd

4th

5th

Finish pickups.

Offer currency packs.

Return to departure centre.

Meet any remainder of group.

Offer them currency packs.

Pick up currency packs, distribute to group, suggest they check contents. Then depart.

0700: Depart departure centre for ferry. Welcome all clients together – introduce self and driver again – do customs forms and fax list before arrival in Dover.

0930: Arrive port of Dover.

1030: Usual sailing from port of Dover.

1300: Arrive at Calais after putting clock one hour forward.

1500: Stop at last svc before entering Brussels – ring rd.

1530: Depart svc stop.

1615: Arrive at Grand Palace – do orientation and give time for dinner.

1930: Depart Grand Palace.

2000: Arrive at hotel for check in – no dinner included.

NOTE: Other option for day is to go to hotel first, check in, then go to town for dinner – this will depend on driving hours.

- ## DAY TWO:

Brussels to Amsterdam – Monday – Hotel Ibis – airport.

0930: Depart hotel.

1030: Arrive at border.

1100: Depart border.

1230: Arrive Volendam.

1330: Depart Volendam

1400: Arrive cheese and dogs.

1500: Depart cheese and dogs.

1530: Arrive town – do diamonds and have free time.

1830: Depart town for hotel.

1900: Arrive hotel.

2000: Included dinner at hotel then free night.

- DAY THREE:

Amsterdam to Rhineland – Tuesday – Hotel Europa-Ludwigshafen.

0845: Depart hotel.
1230: Arrive Cologne – orientation.
1400: Depart Cologne.
1600: Rhine cruise from Boppard.
1730: Depart Rhine cruise from St. Goar.
1845: Arrive Europa Hotel in Ludwigshafen.
1930: Dinner included at hotel – free night to take a stroll or catch up with postcards.

- DAY FOUR:

Ludwigshafen to Giswil (approximately 30 minutes drive from Lake Lucerne) Wednesday – Hotel Krone – Giswil.

0730: Depart hotel.
0800: Arrive Heidelberg – orientation.
0900: Depart Heidelberg.
1100: Arrive svc stop.
1120: Depart svc stop.
1300: Arrive Hofgut Sternen in Helental for lunch and cuckoo clock demo – call for demo.
1415: Depart Hofgut Sternen.
1530: Arrive border.
1545: Depart border.
1615: Arrive Rhinefalls – orientation.
1645: Depart Rhinefalls.
1900: Arrive Giswil.
2000: Dinner.

- ## DAY FIVE:
Giswil (Lucerne at leisure) Thursday.
0800: Depart hotel for Lucerne – optionals possible.
1700: Depart Lucerne for hotel.
1930: Dinner.

- ## DAY SIX:
Giswil to Innsbruck – Friday – Hotel Bon Alpina.
0730: Depart hotel – heavy traffic going around Lucerne.
1000: Arrive Lichtenstein – Vaduz.
1045: Depart Lichtenstein.
1115: Depart border.
1300: Arrive lunch stop.
1345: Depart lunch stop.
1500: Arrive Innsbruck – orientation.
1730: Depart Innsbruck.
1800: Arrive hotel.
1900: Dinner included at hotel.

- ## DAY SEVEN:
Innsbruck to Vienna – Saturday – Hotel Rosen Kavalier.
0900: Depart hotel.
1115: Arrive Berchtesgaden – give story of Berchtesgaden – orientation.
1315: Depart Berchtesgaden.
1515: Arrive svc stop.
1545: Depart svc stop.
1800: Arrive Vienna hotel – no dinner included – optional possible.

- ## DAY EIGHT:

Vienna – Sunday.

0800: Depart hotel for optional imperial highlights.

0810: Meet guide at Schonbrunn palace.

0930: Depart hotel with anyone not doing optional.

0940: Everybody together – departs front gates of Schonbrunn Palace for included sightseeing with local guide – included sightseeing normally finishes at Albertina Platz.

1100: Group has free time to explore Vienna – have lunch – shop – visit other museums etc – also the remainder of the imperial highlights will be conducted at this time.

1500: Depart Vienna – people are normally a little tired by this time.

1530: Arrive at Kavalier hotel – optional possible.

- ## DAY NINE:

Vienna to Venice – Monday – Hotel Holiday Mestre.

0800: Depart hotel.

1030: Arrive svcs.

100: Depart svcs.

1330: Arrive lunch stop.

1430: Depart lunch stop.

1700: Arrive Venice – Hotel Holiday.

1900: Dinner included at hotel – NOTE: This hotel has the ability to serve 50 patrons in under 45 minutes and on a good day I have seen them do it in 30 mins. However sometimes it is not always the 50 people in your group but whatever 50 were sitting in the restaurant. Make sure you are there for the start of dinner or it could all end in tears. Possible optional tonight.

- ## DAY TEN:

Venice – Tuesday

0800:   Depart hotel for boat.

0830:   Arrive Tronchetto for boat.

0845:   Boat departs.

0915:   Boat arrives at Venice waterfront near Metropole Hotel approximately 400 metres from St. Mark's square.

0945:   Arrive St. Mark's Square by foot.

1000:   Arrive glass blowing demonstration Veechia Murano.

1800:   Boat departs Venice.

1830:   Boat arrives Tronchetto.

1900:   Arrive hotel.

2000:   Included dinner at hotel – group is free for day until boat returns to mainland for transfer to hotel – possible optionals today.

- ## DAY ELEVEN:

Venice to Rome – Wednesday – Hotel Grand Fleming.

0730:   Depart Venice.

0930:   Arrive svcs.

1000:   Depart svcs.

1200:   Arrive lunch stop.

1300:   Depart lunch stop.

1530:   Arrive Hotel Fleming. Group has free night – no dinner is included – possible to do optionals – hotel has decent dining facilities or there are several others within the vicinity of the hotel.

- ## DAY TWELVE:

Rome – Thursday.

0700: Many groups will depart for Roman highlights optional, i.e. start at Vatican museum and Sistine Chapel.

0745: Meet local guide at Vatican Museum entrance.

0900: Depart hotel with second group to meet with others at holy door to St. Peter's.

1000: Meet together with remainder of group at holy door of St. Peter's to begin included sightseeing day – will then continue to include other half of Roman highlights as well as the included sightseeing – quite common times are as follows.

1200: Depart St. Peter's coach parking.

1245: Arrive at Colloseum for included sightseeing – then to Roman Forum.

1400: Depart for other half of Roman highlights.

1530: Pick up others from whatever designated meeting point is available on the day.

1600: Arrive at hotel – group has free night – no dinner included so possible optionals.

- ## DAY THIRTEEN:

Great day today to do with what you please – possible free day for group to relax. You may take the opportunity to experience yet more of the wonderful sights of Rome – no dinner is included tonight.

• DAY FOURTEEN

Rome to Bay of Naples – Saturday – Hotel in Stabia, near to Pompeii.

0730: Depart hotel – traffic is normally not bad.

0930: Possible bathroom stop before arriving at Naples.

1100: Approximately – boats to Capri – this will be confirmed with Sireon Tours prior to arrival.

1800: Approximately – return to Naples and head for hotel – can be difficult to find – feel free to call the hotel and ask them to come to the Pompeii exit so that you can follow them if you are not sure – the hotel is in the middle of nowhere but has nice rooms with good air-conditioning and they are eager to please – best to undersell a little bit and clients should be impressed with the included dinner and hospitality of the staff – but do prepare clients as there is very little for them to do in this area.

• DAY FIFTEEN:

Naples to Florence – Sunday – Hotel Moderno Pontessieve.

0730: Depart hotel.

0930: Arrive svc stop.

1000: Depart svc stop.

1200: Arrive lunch stop.

1300: Depart lunch stop.

1500: Arrive Florence – Piazzale Michaelangelo – possible group photo – also can give group time for shopping and sightseeing as well.

1800: Depart Florence.

1830: Arrive hotel – dinner included at hotel – free night to relax, catch up with postcards or such.

- DAY SIXTEEN:

Florence to Nice – Monday – super heavy traffic if staying south of Florence – Hotel Busby.
0730: Depart hotel.
0830: Arrive Florence.
1030: Depart Florence.
1200: Arrive Pisa.
1330: Depart Pisa.
1530: Arrive svcs.
1600: Depart svcs.
1830: Arrive Nice – possible to do orientation on way in as it frees up clients time a little more for the next day.
2000: Included dinner then free night.

- DAY SEVENTEEN:

Nice at leisure – Tuesday.
Possible optional in the morning to do St. Paul de Venceze, village perfumery and a lunch somewhere normally takes approximately seven hours.
1745: Depart for Monte Carlo.
1830: Arrive Monte Carlo – no included dinner tonight – clients may wish to dine in Monte Carlo.
2045: Depart Monte Carlo – return to Nice.
2130: Arrive Nice.

- DAY EIGHTEEN.

Nice to Lyon – Wednesday – Hotel Tulip Inn Saphire.

0730: Depart Hotel.

0830: Arrive Cannes.

0930: Depart Cannes.

1130: Arrive svc stop.

1200: Depart svc stop.

1300: Arrive Avignon – clients enjoy lunch here as they can get a cheap baguette, and stroll around the shops – they enjoy plenty of time in Avignon as they generally prefer the small town to big cities.

1500: Depart Avignon.

1700: Arrive svc stop just before Lyon (in case of traffic).

1720: Depart svc stop.

1830: Hopefully arrive at hotel.

1930: Dinner included – free night to explore Lyon.

- ## DAY NINETEEN:

Lyon to Paris – Thursday – Hotel Ibis Porte de Bercy.

0730: Depart Lyon – the traffic is horrendous if you are south of the tunnel – your group will understand this by now.

0930: Arrive svc stop.

1000: Depart svc stop.

1200: Arrive lunch stop.

1300: Depart lunch stop.

1500: Arrive hotel – hotel is right next to a huge shopping centre so clients can go exploring – Group has free night – no included dinner or sightseeing tonight so possible for optionals to be offered.

- ## DAY TWENTY:

Paris at leisure – Friday.

0745:   Depart hotel for included sightseeing.

0815:   Arrive Notre Dame.

0915:   Depart Notre Dame.

1100:   Arrive Arc de Triumph – finish of included sightseeing – remainder of day can be structured as you like to offer optional visits to museums or points of interest as per suggested itinerary.

1530:   Coach departs town to return to hotel.

1600:   Arrive hotel – free night with no included dinner – possibly do cabaret, or dinner, or illuminations.

- ## DAY TWENTY ONE:

Paris at leisure – Saturday. No scheduled program – as per Rome itinerary.

- ## DAY TWENTY TWO:

Paris to London – Sunday.

Before departing Paris suggest all clients check whereabouts of their passports – depart Paris to co-ordinate with any airport drop offs or rendezvous you may have to make with other tour directors.

General information however …

Paris to Calais is approximately 267km and is usually done with one service stop en route – allow plenty of time for check in prior to sailing – sailing time is 1 hour and 30 minutes – allow one hour to clear customs at Dover or do prior clearance form in your documents and fax in plenty of time to arrive so customs can process – Dover to London travel time approximately 2 hours – thank all your clients on behalf of the Company for choosing to travel with them – do drop-offs and then head for home if you have one, your hotel if you don't – congratulate yourself on another successful tour – then sit back and relax.

What to do in case of an emergency.

- EMERGENCY SERVICES PHONE NUMBER

A lot of people don't realize that no matter where you are in the world emergency services can be accessed on a mobile telephone by pressing the 'plus' symbol followed by the number 112. This will connect you immediately to the emergency service of the country where you are reading this and you should find someone who speaks your language who can help you.

- COACH ACCIDENT WHERE DRIVER AND GUIDE ARE INCAPACITATED.

In the event of a coach accident involving any form of transport where the driver and guide are incapacitated you should telephone emergency services immediately. Also contact the head office of the travel company to put them in the picture. If you do not have this number you can call any travel agent anywhere in the world and they will pass on the relevant information to the head office of your travel company. If you are not travelling with a large tour company the idea would be to contact the travel agency who initially sold you the tour.

- **ROAD ACCIDENT WHERE YOU OR YOUR TRAVELLING COMPANION ARE INJURED.**

With any road accident or emergency situation where a person is injured or incapacitated call emergency services immediately. If no substantial injuries have been sustained and you are travelling in your own, or in a hire car, you should complete a road accident report. This is merely a statement of what you believe to be the facts, and not an admission of guilt. It should be done in duplicate. Both parties write out one of these reports and can use them later to support any claim they might make to an insurance company. These forms will generally accompany car hire documents.

Should anyone require hospitalization make sure medical staff have contact details for yourself, your tour guide, and your travel company.

- **NEED A LOO.**

If at any time you urgently need to visit a bathroom never be afraid to enter a hotel or restaurant and ask to be guided to the café or bar section of the establishment. Provided you purchase some kind of drink you are regarded as a patron and therefore entitled to us the washroom facilities.

- **BEEN ROBBED.**

In the unfortunate even of being robbed while on your holiday your first step should be to report the incident to the nearest police station. Then as quickly as possible you should then endeavour to cancel credit and charge cards to minimize your liability of any unlawful usage of them. Of course you will be carrying on your person detail of the cards recorded on a piece of paper or computer disc before you left home.

- **FALLEN DOWN AND INJURED.**

If you do fall down don't try to get up too quickly. Take stock of things. Get your bearings. Take your time. Determine whether you are injured in any way. And before you know it people will be popping up out of nowhere to assist you.

If you are on your own stay put until someone does come by to help. Allow them to assist you to a seat so that you can regain your composure. Don't feel embarrassed. Take as long as you need until you feel comfortable enough to move on again.

If you are on your own and your injury is more serious, give medical staff, or the first person to arrive, a contact number of someone who needs to be informed of the event. Someone you can rely on to look after your interests.

If you are travelling with someone who falls and is injured you may find it necessary to go to the hospital with them. The best course is to travel in the ambulance with the injured person to soothe and comfort them. Whether there is one person missing from the touring party or two, it really doesn't matter. Although a call to the tour leader would be the considerate thing to do at this stage.

Even better would be to ask the paramedics or a doctor at accident and emergency to do the talking. The story coming from them would be much more detailed and accurate.

Taking an overview, try not to panic in any emergency situation. Stay calm and take stock of things. If there are several of you, stay together. Don't split up. Help each other.

• RIPPED OFF BY TAXI DRIVER.

When getting into any taxi try to obtain a business card of the taxi firm, or at the very least, get the name of the company. Write down the number of the taxi – they all have one – plus the telephone number prominently displayed on the car somewhere. If you feel you have been grossly over-charged for a trip ring your hotel and describe the journey to them. They may possibly phone the taxi company on your behalf to find out whether you have in fact been charged too much. Or you can phone the Company yourself.

What you can do to avoid all this sort of thing though is to agree on a price for the journey before you actually get into the taxi. Establish whether the amount you have been told is for one person, or all your party. Whether in fact it includes luggage and boundary charges. You are after a complete all-inclusive price, and when you get it, write it on the card and get the driver to agree that it is correct before continuing.

Precautionary measures that could save you thousands.

- ## ALWAYS WRITE DOWN THE NUMBER OF TAXIS YOU HAVE TRAVELLED IN.

While on holiday write down the number of every taxi you travel in. The reason for this is that if you leave behind anything of value in one of these vehicles you'll know where to start looking for it. If it is something valuable such as a handbag, wallet or camera you may have to resign yourself to the fact that you will never see it again. But taking the number of the taxi gives you a fighting change of getting it back.

- ## REMOVAL OF LUGGAGE FROM TAXIS.

Never close the doors of a taxi until you are absolutely sure you have all your luggage from both the boot or trunk and from the inside of the vehicle. Sometimes at the end of a taxi journey people jump out, pay the driver, and in their excitement go to the rear of the vehicle where they stand waiting for the driver to open the boot for them. But the driver sees the passenger shutting the door behind them and assumes it is safe to drive away, forgetting whether this particular fare may or may not have had luggage.

I always suggest to people that they pay the taxi driver last. Although in some countries the driver will expect to be paid before the passengers leave the car. But removal of all your belongings before payment is still the safest course no matter what the driver says.

Wherever you are always make sure you use taxis belonging to registered taxi companies. In some countries there are ruthless operators who might take you to somewhere such as the airport, charge an extortionate fee, then refuse to get your luggage out for you until you have paid.

If staying at a hotel get the concierge to call you a taxi. Don't take your luggage to the edge of the footpath and try hailing your own. You might be picked up by a rogue operator and asked to pay double or triple the normal fare.

Another trick to be wary of is that of getting the correct change. Or more precisely, **not** getting the correct change. When you've agreed on a price with the driver to take you to the airport make sure you have the exact amount ready to give him. It's remarkable how often high value notes have been given by the passenger in payment of a ride only to be told by the driver that he has 'run out of change'.

You are in a hurry. Your plane will be leaving in less than an hour. You've agreed on a price of 35 pounds for the taxi to take you from central London to Heathrow airport and all you have on you is a 50 pound note. Your natural response is to argue and express your point of view that it should be the responsibility of the driver to have change, but in the end you leave the change remembering not to fall into the same trap another time.

- **SECRET HIDING PLACES.**

The problem with secret hiding places is that sometimes they can be so secret you are likely to forget where you may have planted a valuable item. Don't put your money under a hotel mattress, for example. In the haste of departure many have left the building and forgotten all about their cash. Others aren't keen to take their valuables on a day trip somewhere, or on a shopping expedition, and might stuff them behind a TV set, or at the back of a drawer. These are not good ideas. If on a rare occasion crooks enter your room during your absence just remember that they know all these hiding places better than you do.

- **TAKING BUSINESS CARDS FROM ESTABLISHMENTS YOU HAVE PATRONIZED.**

Always take a business card from restaurants you've dined in and hotels you have patronized. So that if by chance you do leave something of value behind in one of these places you can call to retrieve it. Most importantly however the first thing you should ask for is the manager and their name before you let anyone know you left your wallet with a thousand dollars in cash down the side of the seat in the restaurant. The best thing to do is return in person if at all possible.

- **NEVER OPEN YOUR WALLET OR PURSE IN PUBLIC.**

Don't ever flash your money. You never know who may be watching. Find a quiet area to open your wallet where there is less chance of being observed by people of criminal intent.

In any event it's best to carry no more than about 50 euro at any one time. Plus a credit card for any possible major purchases.

When paying by credit card always keep it in sight. Unscrupulous shop owners have been known to take peoples' cards out the back somewhere and run off extra slips with them. You sign one at the front of the shop and your genuine signature is used to forge the others. There is really no need for a shopkeeper to take your card away.

If you are offered a free sight-seeing tour by anyone in a car or on a motorbike just say 'no'. One way or the other you will be the loser. There are dozens of little scams which end up with you losing your money or your bag, and the other person never being seen again.

6

COMING HOME

The last couple of days.

If you are coming into the last two or three days of a coach tour it is always worth while to have a good look at your suitcase and dispose of anything that you don't really need to take any further. On one of your last free nights toss out any newspapers or brochures you've managed to accumulate, and also any clothing you brought along but never used. Upon reflection you suddenly realize you never wear those particular items at home anyway so this is definitely the time to throw them out. You don't need to take any of this stuff home with you at all.

So earmark the items for charity. Give them to the hotel to pass on to people who can put them to better use. Why clog up your cupboards back home? This is also a good time to check that all your documentation is in order. And to ensure that your car and house keys are not too far away.

I once returned to my home after a tour to find that I had left my house keys in the last hotel I'd stayed at. It was an expensive lesson. It cost me almost 200 pounds to have the locks replaced on the house and for a locksmith to come and let me in. So when coming to the conclusion of your tour check all these things and make sure nothing is missing.

Another reason for doing this is that once everything is checked and found to be in order you can sit back and relax and enjoy the last few days of your tour.

Also, with ever changing regulations on aircraft, you need to be very conscious of excessive luggage on the plane. But because you lightened your suitcase considerably you won't get charged for extra weight. It'll be one less thing you have to worry about.

Keeping in touch.

At the conclusion of any significant holiday together many people will have exchanged addresses with one another. But while these people may have had all sorts of wonderful intentions of keeping in touch later, the reality is somewhat different. The good intentions begin to dwindle away or disappear as everyone gets back to their own day to day routines. And nothing comes of all the address gathering.

But it is well worthwhile to keep in touch with the people you made friends with on the tour. Maintaining contact will enable you to continue experiencing different cultures around the world and should you decide to travel again some time in the future you'll have a list of like-minded people to visit and to plan further trips with.

From my experience I have had many people who maintained very good relationships from the other side of the world. They have travelled on a regular basis together from such far-flung countries as America, Canada, New Zealand, Australia, South Africa, Singapore, The Philippines, and many other countries all over the world to a common meeting point from which they all shared further travel experiences.

These days, with the ease of keeping in touch through the use of e-mail, telephones and letters, there is no reason not to keep in touch. And if you're not familiar with the e-mail system it is well worth spending time learning it. A whole new world can open up for you in this way. Electronic communication is the way of the future, so why hold back. Learn this new skill because there are endless benefits for both you and your old travelling friends.

After the tour.

At the conclusion of your tour when you get back home, the people and events of the last few weeks or so might tend to become one large blur in your mind. And you may slowly start forgetting people and their names, and incidents and where they occurred. But it needn't be that way.

There are a lot of little things you can do to keep the holiday fresh in your mind over the coming years.

We've already covered some of them. You may have been keeping a journal each day or filling in a day planner with memory-jogging facts. You have various photographs taken along the way and the group photo itself with everyone's names written down, together with their addresses.

You would have made special friends with several people in the group, you have their photo so you won't forget what they look like, you have their addresses, so the next obvious thing to do after coming home is to keep in touch with these people. Because you don't know what the future holds. You may journey to their country one day and share many a laugh. Or you may choose to go on another tour together and enjoy each others' company in some different part of the world. And on this new adventure you will want to take photographs and keep a journal again to maintain a record of the event.

The journal, the day planner, and all your photographs are a tangible record of the good times. So that in the future when visited by a person who was in your tour group you can bring it all out and enjoy re-living them all over again.

Sometimes on a tour you may have had your photograph taken with various locals in the countries visited and promised them that upon your return home you would send them this, that or the other thing. It's very important to honour any promises made on your holiday. There may or may not be a future payoff. It doesn't really matter. What does matter is that you should let your word mean something even though you may never see the person again. People in the hospitality industry are tickled pink to receive a card or e-mail from people they've dealt with, especially when these messages come from the other side of the world. And who knows. It might be the start of something beautiful. You might gain a lifelong pen pal. You might even gain a true friend. So if you've promised to send a photograph, or to stay in touch, do so without delay upon returning home. It's the decent thing to do.

Likewise with members of your tour group. It's quite natural for you to have bonded with some of these people and communication is a great strengthener of bonds. You have all shared something in common and as friendships develop you'll quite likely find that you have other things in common too. So drop them a line, keep in touch, and don't hesitate to send out regular cards, letters and e-mails.

I have people who still send me cards at Christmas and occasional e-mails after fifteen years of knowing them. Over that time I've built up a network of hundreds of contacts all over the world simply by keeping in touch. It's always nice to hear from them, and learn what they're up to, and how their lives are going, and the last thing I want is to lose contact with them.

I think it is a shame sometimes when people go away to the other side of the world and have a fantastic time then come back home and not keep in touch with people. After a time things fade from mind and it's almost as though the holiday never happened. So don't let this happen to you.

Your tour may have cost you several thousand dollars and you need to get your money's worth. You need to keep the memories alive and on tap to share with others. Your tour company and tour director gave you the materials to have a good holiday. They gave you the canvas, the brushes and the paints. It was up to you what kind of a holiday picture you painted. And having completed your picture, are you then going to hide it away in a cupboard when you get home? Of course not. You'll want to display it for others to see and to be a constant reminder of where you went, what you saw, and the people you met.

7

THINGS TO PHOTOCOPY

The following few pages have been included for you to photocopy ....

List of films used (4 rolls of 36 photos).

	FILM 1	FILM 2	FILM 3	FILM 4
1				
2				
3				
4				
5				
6				
7				
8				
9				
10				
11				
12				
13				
14				
15				
16				
17				
18				
19				
20				
21				
22				
23				
24				

25				
26				
27				
28				
29				
30				
31				
32				
33				
34				
35				
36				

Day Planner

CITY	DATE
DAY	THINGS TO DO
WAKE UP	1
BREAKFAST	2
BAGS	3
DEPART 1	4
DEPART 2	5

EVENING   PURCHASES
DEPART
DINNER

NOTES

MUST REMEMBER

PRICELESS MOMENT

CITY	DATE
DAY	THINGS TO DO
WAKE UP	1
BREAKFAST	2
BAGS	3
DEPART 1	4
DEPART 2	5

EVENING   PURCHASES
DEPART
DINNER

NOTES

MUST REMEMBER

PRICELESS MOMENT

CITY	DATE
DAY	THINGS TO DO
WAKE UP	1
BREAKFAST	2
BAGS	3
DEPART 1	4
DEPART 2	5

EVENING   PURCHASES
DEPART
DINNER

NOTES

MUST REMEMBER

PRICELESS MOMENT

CITY	DATE
DAY	THINGS TO DO
WAKE UP	1
BREAKFAST	2
BAGS	3
DEPART 1	4
DEPART 2	5

EVENING   PURCHASES
DEPART
DINNER

NOTES

MUST REMEMBER

PRICELESS MOMENT

Day Planner

CITY	**DATE**
DAY	**THINGS TO DO**
WAKE UP	**1**
BREAKFAST	**2**
BAGS	**3**
DEPART 1	**4**
DEPART 2	**5**

EVENING   **PURCHASES**
DEPART
DINNER

NOTES

MUST REMEMBER

PRICELESS MOMENT

CITY	**DATE**
DAY	**THINGS TO DO**
WAKE UP	**1**
BREAKFAST	**2**
BAGS	**3**
DEPART 1	**4**
DEPART 2	**5**

EVENING   **PURCHASES**
DEPART
DINNER

NOTES

MUST REMEMBER

PRICELESS MOMENT

CITY	**DATE**
DAY	**THINGS TO DO**
WAKE UP	**1**
BREAKFAST	**2**
BAGS	**3**
DEPART 1	**4**
DEPART 2	**5**

EVENING   **PURCHASES**
DEPART
DINNER

NOTES

MUST REMEMBER

PRICELESS MOMENT

CITY	**DATE**
DAY	**THINGS TO DO**
WAKE UP	**1**
BREAKFAST	**2**
BAGS	**3**
DEPART 1	**4**
DEPART 2	**5**

EVENING   **PURCHASES**
DEPART
DINNER

NOTES

MUST REMEMBER

PRICELESS MOMENT

Contact and address list.

NAME:
....
ADDRESS:.....................
....
....
....
....
....

NAME:
....
ADDRESS:.....................
....
....
....
....
....

NAME:
....
ADDRESS:.....................
....
....
....
....
....

NAME:
....
ADDRESS:.....................
....
....
....
....
....

NAME:
....
ADDRESS:.....................
....
....
....
....
....

NAME:
....
ADDRESS:.....................
....
....
....
....
....

NAME:
....
ADDRESS:.....................
....
....
....
....
....

NAME:
....
ADDRESS:.....................
....
....
....
....
....

Contact and address list.

NAME:	NAME:
....	....
ADDRESS:.....................	ADDRESS:.....................
....	....
....	....
....	....
....	....
....	....
NAME:	**NAME:**
....	....
ADDRESS:.....................	ADDRESS:.....................
....	....
....	....
....	....
....	....
....	....
NAME:	**NAME:**
....	....
ADDRESS:.....................	ADDRESS:.....................
....	....
....	....
....	....
....	....
....	....
NAME:	**NAME:**
....	....
ADDRESS:.....................	ADDRESS:.....................
....	....
....	....
....	....
....	....
....	....

Movies to watch to get you in the mood.

'National Lampoon European Vacation'

- A funny look at Europe and many of its countries and if you don't see it before you go you definitely must see it when you return.

'Room with a View'

- To get a feel for Florence.

'Waterloo'

- The story of Napoleon. It will show you why the French admired him so greatly.

'Roman Holiday'

- A movie to get you in the mood for Rome. Will show you many of the famous sights.

'Ben Hur'

- If you like a bit of spice, and appreciate a bit of action, this movie is bigger than Rome itself. Even today the scene of the chariot race would still rate as one of the great pieces of cinematography.

'Only You'

- With Marisa Tomei and Robert Downey jnr will give you a lighthearted look at Italy from Venice to Tuscany on to Rome and the Amalfi Coast. A lighthearted comedy/romance.

'El Cid'

- Should you be heading to Spain?

'Dirty Rotten Scoundrels'

- If you are heading for the French Riviera and Monaco this movie has some very enjoyable scenery as well as a good mix of British, American and French humour.

'Ronan'

- If you are looking for a great action movie set in France and featuring Robert de Niro look no further. The car chase on the periphery of Paris will make your head spin.

EMERGENCY CONTACT LIST 'A'.

YOUR NAME:..

ADDRESS:

....

....

....

TRAVEL INSURANCE COMPANY:...

POLICY NO:...

CONTACT NO:..

LOST CREDIT CARDS – CONTACT DETAILS:

CREDIT CARD COMPANY:...

PHONE NO:..

E-MAIL:...

CREDIT CARD COMPANY:...

PHONE NO:..

E-MAIL:...

CREDIT CARD COMPANY:...

PHONE NO:..

E-MAIL:...

EMERGENCY CONTACT PERSON – (APART FROM NEXT OF KIN).

NAME:...

WORK PH:...

HOME PH:.............................MOBILE PH:..............................

EMAIL:..

EMERGENCY CONTACT LIST 'B'.

DOCTOR: ....

WORK PH: ....

HOME PH: ....

MOBILE PH: ....

EMAIL: ....

CHECK OUT THAT YOUR WILL IS UP TO DATE MAKE SURE ANYONE WHO HAS NOT BEEN NICE TO YOU FOR THE LAST YEAR IS WRITTEN OUT JUST IN CASE (HA HA!)

LAWYERS DETAILS:
WORK PH: ....

HOME PH: ....

MOBILE PH: ....

EMAIL: ....

TRAVEL AGENT DETAILS:
WORK PH: ....

HOME PH: ....

MOBILE PH: ....

EMAIL: ....

PASSPORT DETAILS

PHOTOCOPY OR DIGITAL PHOTO OF THE MAIN INFORMATION PAGE AS WELL AS ANY VISAS YOU HAVE

NEXT OF KIN LIST:

PREFERENCE 1: .... PREFERENCE 2: ....

WORK PH: .... WORK PH: ....

HOME PH: .... HOME PH: ....

MOBILE PH: .... MOBILE PH: ....

EMAIL: .... EMAIL: ....

LORELEI

I cannot divine what it meaneth,
This haunting nameless pain:
A tale of the bygone ages
Keeps brooding through my brain:

The faint air cools in the gloaming,
And peaceful flows the Rhine,
The thirsty summits are drinking
The sunset's flooding wine;

The loveliest maiden is sitting
High-throned in yon blue air,
Her golden jewels are shining,
She combs her golden hair;

She combs with a comb that is golden,
And sings a weird refrain
That steeps in a deadly enchantment
The list'ner's ravished brain:

The doomed in his drifting shallop,
Is tranced with the sad sweet tone,
He sees not the yawning breakers,
He see but the maid alone:

The pitiless billows engulf him! –
So perish sailor and bark;
And this with her baleful singing,
Is the Lorelei's gruesome work.

By Heinrich Heine

Loreley-Lied (1822)

Translated by

Mark Twain (S.L. Clemens) in 'A Tramp Abroad'
(1800)

TRAVEL JOURNAL

TRAVEL JOURNAL

TRAVEL JOURNAL

TRAVEL JOURNAL

TRAVEL JOURNAL

TRAVEL JOURNAL

TRAVEL JOURNAL

TRAVEL JOURNAL

TRAVEL JOURNAL

TRAVEL JOURNAL

TRAVEL JOURNAL

TRAVEL JOURNAL

TRAVEL JOURNAL

TRAVEL JOURNAL

TRAVEL JOURNAL

TRAVEL JOURNAL

TRAVEL JOURNAL

TRAVEL JOURNAL

TRAVEL JOURNAL

TRAVEL JOURNAL

TRAVEL JOURNAL

TRAVEL JOURNAL

TRAVEL JOURNAL

TRAVEL JOURNAL

TRAVEL JOURNAL

TRAVEL JOURNAL

TRAVEL JOURNAL

TRAVEL JOURNAL

TRAVEL JOURNAL

TRAVEL JOURNAL

TRAVEL JOURNAL

TRAVEL JOURNAL

TRAVEL JOURNAL

TRAVEL JOURNAL

TRAVEL JOURNAL

TRAVEL JOURNAL

TRAVEL JOURNAL

TRAVEL JOURNAL

TRAVEL JOURNAL

TRAVEL JOURNAL

TRAVEL JOURNAL

TRAVEL JOURNAL

TRAVEL JOURNAL

TRAVEL JOURNAL